The Missing Pieces

A Reflection on Operational Efficiency

Jean Gaël Le Flem
Bertrand Oliva

The Missing Pieces

A Reflection on Operational Efficiency

Translated into English
by Nafkote Tamirat

éditions de l'école de guerre

Collection
Honni soit qui mal y pense

Note from the publisher

Ecole de guerre – the French War College – is a place of study and reflection that shapes tomorrow's leaders for the next Trojan War or the next Hundred, Thirty or Seven Years' Wars. Our battles no longer take place in an arena within the palisades of an enclosed ground; and they concern not just those in uniform serving their country, soulless mercenaries or the lost child-soldiers of the melancholic tropics. These combats are the common responsibility of our democracies. Study and reflection cannot be the only outcome from officers developing their thinking in this timeless quadrangle that the Ecole Militaire would be if it did not open up to the world.

Herein lies the vocation of the Ecole de Guerre Publications: to spark intelligence, foster writing and publish for the benefit of reflection and dialogue for all, civilian or military.

This publishing house does not disseminate official doxa – other channels exist for that; it does not even represent War College doctrine. It simply wishes to make public works which, controversial or not, are the opinion only of their authors yet will contribute to French military, geopolitical and strategic thinking.

For that it is based on four collections:

- "*Champs de bataille*" deals with history, geopolitics and strategy;

- "*Ligne de front*" illustrates this need to think differently, a leitmotif of the French War College;

- "*Feux croisés*" addresses realities and parallel or indeed divergent issues;

- "*Honni soit qui mal y pense*" publishes texts written in English with a French way of thinking.

Preface

To many observers, the traditional European schools of military theory prevalent in the 18th and 19th centuries have all but disappeared. The Prussian, French, British and Italian schools of war – each having a very different approach to the conduct of war and military interventions – appeared to mutate and merge together during the 20th Century to become a single Western Way of War: Expeditionary military intervention, with distinct causes and lines of victory. Today, most military officers in their professional military education examine The Cold War as the greatest single achievement of this Western Way of War: Technology and precision deterring and the defeating the combined (and more numerous) forces of the Warsaw pact. It could be argued that from there until today, the West simply adopted a unified theory or approach to war and warfare that it has applied to every conflict since 1970.

Yet as this work by Le Flem and Oliva shows a potential reawakening of true intellectual analysis and thinking in Europe, undistracted by the fads of Strategic Autonomy, Tailored Deterrence or Multi Domain Operations. They tackle the fallacies of a militarised counter-terror policy, the illusion of value in Comprehensive Approaches, and the mythology of decapitation strategies, as well as the campaign failures of military interventions with equal aplomb. Their desire to develop a new (or at least reimagined) operational and strategic design for the use of militaries in delivering foreign policy is audacious and courageous.

In addressing such an ambitious goal, Le Flem and Oliva deviate from the orthodoxy: they openly mock the spin and propaganda of government policy, business speak, grand narratives and pontification. They self-identify with the usual strategy answers provided by academic or military courses and literature – that of the easy broad principles, the trendy, and the demagogy, and deliberately avoid such pitfalls. In doing so, they observe with chilling accuracy the tendency of many analysts to simply blame failure on poor strategy, and recommend different processes, policy and people. Unusually, they also accept that bureaucracy has a role in forming policy and strategy, as well as in militaries.

Instead, the authors cut to the soul of theoretical arguments, redefining efficiency (for native English speakers read 'efficacy'), and complexity in an accessible way that is actually useful to policy and decision-makers. The analysis of ideological trends is worthy of a debate with Noah Yuri Harari, and their understanding and articulation of the political-military divide is peerless.

Such where does this clarity of thought and incisive wit lead Le Flem and Oliva? In part their approach of blending of Clausewitz, Sun Tsu and Beaufre is not new (nor do they claim it to be). Aligning activity to political goals is a well-trodden path. But the authors go much further, in pressing for a more dynamic approach across all aspects of the strategy making equation, and in the implementation of policy direction and decisions. The need to accept and welcome the perpetual evolution of political objectives alongside military activity should herald a new era in adaptive strategy and operations.

Underpinning this, one detects the heart of the infantry officer on operations – with clear advocacy for an audacity of planning and acting that embraces complexity and the spirit of élan. It is truly a return to the French school of war. And that is perhaps the most exciting part of this book. There are few military officers across Europe who would be brave enough to write a publication such as this, because political commanders will not appreciate being upstaged by officers who think more deeply and clearly than their superiors. It is enormous credit to the Ecole de Guerre that minds such as Le Flem and Oliva have been awakened by an enlightened leadership.

What we have before us might well be the return of thinking in modern European militaries. One can only hope that others have the courage to follow.

Professor Peter Roberts
7 January 2019

Preface – French Edition

Why, for fifteen years, have large nations felt helpless in their attempts to establish sustainable peace in regions left ruined by violence, where their armed forces are engaged in the name of that ever elusive "international community"?

As our University questions itself and feels its way forward, tempted by the radical act of challenging the very principle of military intervention, Jean Gaël Le Flem and Bertrand Oliva thoughtfully break down the mechanism of failure, offer a new kind of strategic approach and blaze a forward to a regained efficiency. With the audacity and impertinence of their age and generation, these two trainee officers of the École de Guerre methodically criticize the conventional politico-military patterns, as well as the simplifying slogans of counter-terrorism and counterinsurgency, while citing Sun Tzu and Beaufre, in order to suggest a pioneering approach towards the conflicts of our times. Their analyses are reinforced by their own personal experiences in these wars, which anchor them in the reality of the field, and by the expectations of the peoples who suffer the consequences.

This brilliant essay is one of the most enticing works I've been given to read in the last ten years. Combining analytic rigor and outspokenness, it opens doors, sometimes old and forgotten, far from the pre-packaged thinking that too often dominates the decision-making circles of large international organizations. Not least among its merits is how it restores political action and diplomacy to a primary position in the management of the complexity that characterizes these situations, where the line between war and peace gets blurred.

Jean Gaël Le Flem and Bertrand Oliva brilliantly demonstrate here, if we still need the reminder, that today, just like in the past, military actors cannot disregard strategic reflection.

General Henri Bentégeat

Introduction

Our questions about the efficiency of the actions we led during external operations lie at in the very roots of this essay. Having participated in the majority of the operations carried out in the last ten years, we have asked ourselves how the actions led in the field could be effective on a strategic or political level. Clearly, it would be easy to counter that from a perspective so low on the ladder of power, of course it would be difficult to assess the strategic and political consequences of field operations. It's also true an operation might be politically successful, even as, on the ground, troops feel as though their capacities have been underutilized. Nonetheless, one could also argue that these questions have no less of an effect on the strategic community and the political leadership.

Are the operations that we carry out today efficient? First of all, let's not be naïve. The efficiency of an operation is assessed in light of the goals for the war that were decided by politicians. However, those goals are of a different order. Certain are linked with the "official" purposes of the action, like "fighting terrorism in advance" while others refer to the image of itself that

France wants to promote in relation to its international responsibilities, including how it "responds to calls for help from allied country" or "avoids massacre". Finally, certain goals are not made public and fall within a purely political sphere, which looks at national interest in the short, medium and long term. We could stop our reflection right here: we could, trusting and obedient, believe that the military instrument should limit itself to attaining the political objectives it was officially assigned. We could decide that questions about whether or not it's efficient are for the politicians who will make their evaluations by keeping in mind their fixed objectives and their own criteria, which may or may not be communicated outside their circles. And yet, we do not think it useless to reflect upon this question of efficiency. This is firstly because the military is often in a prime position to understand the realities of the geopolitical stakes, the power struggles and the evolution of threats. Secondly, its role is not just that of a tool; it is also an artisan, in the sense that its intelligence and its political sensibilities are fundamental to the continued offering of strategies that are in tune with political ambitions.

This question has become the object of extensive reflection for politicians and intellectuals. They often express a kind of skepticism when it comes to how external interventions might be capable of responding to political issues, one of the questions asked by Dominique de Villepin in his latest book *Mémoire de paix pour temps de guerre*. But these questions can also be found in the Parliamentary accounts of the Assemblée nationale (National Assembly) and the Sénat[1] (Senate), publications from major think tanks and the published work of intellectuals. In the last fifteen years, an entire literature has achieved great success in its contemplation of the "mixed" feelings of political leaders when looking at contemporary military interventions.

It should be noted that the criticism leveled against contemporary external interventions very rarely incriminate the institution of the military itself. The efficiency of soldiers is rarely challenged. In fact, ever since the wave of attacks against our country, our soldiers have probably never looked so good and their professionalism has never been so celebrated. This is why we're less interested in the question of "efficiency in the war" as opposed to that of "the efficiency of war itself", meaning, the ability of external interventions to reach political objectives, when adopting good strategies. The American intervention in Iraq in 2003 and the overthrow of General Gaddafi in Libya in 2011 are of course the most frequently used examples when illustrating the very disappointing track record of external interventions. Perhaps more astonishing is that the intervention of French forces in Mali in December 2013, initially considered a political and military success for France, is seen by many of those same politicians as an example

1. Senate report no. 794. Information report completed in the name of the Committee on Foreign Affairs, the Defense Committee and the Armed Services Committee, to assess external operations. Authors: Messrs. Jacques Gautier, Daniel Reiner, Jean-Marie-Bockel, Jeanny Lorgeoux, Cédric Perrin and Gilbert Roger

of "diminishing returns". The argument that at least the political objectives were achieved (insofar as these objectives remain unknown to the general public) can no longer be accepted: the chaos seen by these countries and the chain reactions of destabilization that these situations produce, discredit in the long-term any country that thought it could resolve the problem and ultimately, was unable to do so.

So, why reflect on the efficiency of external military interventions when well-known researchers and politicians have already explored the subject and considered at length the possibilities and limits of military action? Our goal with this essay is not to develop a comprehensive reflection on conflict, where we write about the strategies which could have been more effective in the past. Instead, we'd like to reflect on how we might improve this efficiency by rooting ourselves in the realities of the today's operations, with which we are familiar.

In his book *Introduction à la stratégie*, General Beaufre lays down a classification of strategic models[2], which are the many kinds of conflict that pit two states against each other. He chooses five models, taking into account the following characteristics: the means that were used, the importance of the issue (the ambition) and the freedom to act. This list is not an exhaustive one and General

2. The five models are the following: powerful means and a modest objective; weak means and a weak objective; limited freedom of action, limited means and an important objective; substantial freedom of action and weak means; substantial military means and substantial freedom of action.

Beaufre encourages the reader to explore further. It seems, today, that a sixth model could be established in order to describe the strategic model of our current engagements: limited ambitions (the absence of immediate vital challenges for France), limited means and a weak freedom to act (as a result of strong constraints from the global environment). This kind of reflection merits completion, as it would help political authorities better understand the reality of what the military might be able to produce in the current setting. This is not about the military expressing a whim to demonstrate its expertise. Rather, it's about the need to break the "dependence of politicians on military solutions that they themselves have not mastered"[3]. This dependence, once insignificant weak when figures like General De Gaulle or Pierre Messmer were in command, has greatly increased as our political leaders are often without any sort of military experience.

Why write this now? The question of war effectiveness is not a new one. In each generation, general staffs struggle to adapt their means and methods to current situations and situations that can be anticipated for the near future. Today, there's a general feeling that we've reached the end of a cycle without ever really understanding the contours of that cycle. The global rearmament of the world's leading nations; western countries' failures in their last counterterror-

3. Dominique de Villepin, *Mémoires de paix pour temps de guerre* (Grasset: 2016)

ism engagements; the question of immigration which is slowly becoming a security issue; the emergence of an increasingly structured kind of terrorism; the annexation of Crimea through a combination of conventional and unconventional methods (the term "hybrid war" is regularly used); the development of technologies whose possible uses we imagine but cannot describe with precision... Threat and war have put on the global agenda, as we live in a time overshadowed by the misleading term "crisis". Faced with this feeling of doubt, politicians, citizens and the military call into question, as they well should, the efficiency of their army and their interventions.

At this sentiment, current strategic changes overlay the western world's ideological shift when it comes to what "use of force" even means. A quick look at the history of international relations allows us to understand that at the heart of these relations, the debate between ideology and realism has always been central and the pendulum is swinging once again towards realism. After the peaceful collapse of the Eastern bloc at the start of the nineties, a new kind of international relations ideology emerged. Strengthened by the famous "end of history" cited by Francis Fukuyama, the western world, and especially the United States, has fallen prey to a certain messianism, perfectly embodied by the neoconservative movement. For them, "humanity holds in its hands the chance to ensure the triumph of liberty over its enemies. The United States is proud of the responsibility that has fallen to it to lead this important mission. [...] We have decided to promote human dignity, freedom of religion and freedom of conscience."[4] This American ideology, which reached its peak with the creationist dream of state building interventions, was initially criticized by France, before it too fell into line with this vision of the world. President Sarkozy signed on in his inauguration speech to the Union pour un Mouvement Populaire (UMP) in January, 2007: "I want to be the president of a human rights France. Each time a woman is martyred in the world, France should be at her side."[5] These words are, certainly, those of a candidate during an election; that does not make them any less the vision of an era, one that did not change during the five-year term of François Hollande. But this era seems over now. National interest, long considered a recollection of nationalism, has once again been claimed. It's no longer "shameful, since the first duty of any government is to defend it" as Tzetan Todorov[6] emphasizes, devoting as he did a large part of his work to fighting the ideological slant of international relations. Even Donald Trump, with his famous slogan, "America First", has officially given up on this messianic American vision: "[...] we will no longer use American military might to construct democracies in faraway lands or try to rebuild other countries in

4. Speech from George W. Bush, September 12, 2002

5. Nicolas Sarkozy during his inauguration speech to the UMP, January 14, 2007

6. Tzetan Todorov, *Le nouveau désordre mondial : réflexions d'un européen* (Robert Laffont, 2003)

our own image. Those days are now over. Instead, we will work with allies and partners to protect our shared interests."[7] President [Emmanuel] Macron also agrees with the American president on this point, as we see in this excerpt from his interview with *Point* on August 23, 2017: "The western world has lost itself in an untimely moral interventionism in the Middle East, as well as in North Africa, during the last ten years. [...] We must end this ill-digested neo-conservatism that leads us to interfere in the domestic policies of others, only to find ourselves then isolated. In Libya and in Syria, this drove us to cruel failures." The question of right, meaning the right of intervention, while not completely excluded in certain extreme cases, seems outmoded now. This renunciation of moral interventionism is an important event in international relations, especially within the framework of reflecting on the efficiency of external interventions. Unfortunately, this twilight of ideology as the main engine of interventions, as reassuring as it might be, does not guarantee the efficiency of new ideas regarding how we use external interventions; instead, it means that we must adapt to them.

Confronted with this world crossed through with new ideological trends, a question arises regarding the efficiency of our strategies, the pertinence of our procedures and the use of our means: is our frame of

7. "We will no longer use American military power to build democracies in faraway countries or to try to rebuild nations in our own image. Those days are over. Instead, we're going to work with our allies and partners to defend our common interests."

reference for the threat posed still valid? This evolution of threats has not been dealt with, neither by the adaptation of methods nor by new intellectual outlines. Western armies thus continue to cling to principles of a comprehensive approach which, in its current sense, serves as a perfect embodiment of western ideology since September 11. This approach, in its original sense, was conceived and put into action in the 2000s as an attempt to better understand the complexity of theaters of operations and to provide a rational framework for western messianic tendencies: it ended by setting itself up as politics and strategy, all at once, when it should have stayed with the question of "how". This approach, whose efficiency has yet to be proven, remains the main dogma to which the United States and its armies cling. They loyally stand by this idea, which holds that armies can rise to the challenges of security, governance and development: they are convinced that efforts made towards civil society guarantee its acceptance of the military presence or rather, the acceptance of local authorities of interference under the guise of helping with governance. The classic objective of achieving "a safe and secure environment"[8] in a few years, in anticipation of "free and democratic elections" seems unattainable; it regularly places armies in situations of failure and does not serve political objectives.

8. This expression became a leitmotif of military operations following the events of September 11, 2001.

This essay will begin with the premise that the efficiency of military interventions relies on the coherence between political ambitions, military objectives, modes of action and agreed upon means. It will determine the best way to reconnect with this coherence in current interventions. It will reflect on how to take into account all the possibilities offered by the evolutions of local situations, rather than looking to impose western visions on other soils. It will then endeavor to reconnect with an approach that reconciles the necessity of returning political meaning to action, adapting to complexity as well as to the unexpected and the need for the military to plan and execute clear objectives. This approach aims to act on the profound tendencies that structure a state and have emerge local options, with the conviction that only internal solutions can be established on a long-lasting basis. This approach constantly seeks out ways to make the best of the evolution of situations, relying as it does on permanent political involvement to guarantee the adapting of military action to the diplomatic road map; the distinction of a time of diplomacy coming after a time of military action is thus abolished. To fight the accusation of interference, it looks to anticipation, the seizing of opportunities and discretion. In direct opposition to the idea of a *continuum* of operations, which conceives of an army intervention as being the necessary prerequisite to diplomatic action, it refuses to separate a military time from a time of diplomacy. In short, relying on the thesis of General Beaufre, it involves, when faced with the unpredictability of situations, looking for the right balance between the need to give oneself a long-term goal, the guarantee of coherence, and the necessity of a responsive adjustment to circumstances.

Before going any further, two caveats. Firstly, if a lot of the thoughts developed in this essay have a general scope to them, this is because we were mostly focusing on weak and medium intensity operations, those that could be encountered in current theaters of operation, notably in Africa and the Middle East. This means that we left out of this analysis high intensity conflicts or, inversely, certain operations that spoke more to the diplomatic situation than a real intervention, as was the case with the engagement in Lebanon, the show of force in the Baltic States or the essentials of the peacekeeping operations. Finally, our infantry officer orientation has inevitably made us prioritize examples on land and unfairly neglect air and sea, which we will sometimes allude to, without sufficiently developing those areas.

The Efficiency of External Interventions: Reality and Perception

In the introduction, we underlined that the efficiency of our external interventions has been regularly met with doubt. In order to avoid all polemics on this fundamental premise, we'll try to establish a specific diagnosis of intervention efficiency, using a precise empirical basis.

The question of subjectivity when it comes to assessments is essential, linked as it to individual "cognitive biases" and the collective "conformity bias". All of the actors in a crisis do not "feel" in the same way, but we will demonstrate that the points of view on this subject often match once passions have died down. This is why we will try to present current interventions as they were perceived by the main actors of the intervening countries (political circles, the army and public opinion) as well as from the viewpoint of the countries in which these interventions took place, what we will call "host countries". Even if this classification of main players is incomplete, it will allow us to establish a complete enough panel of criticism expressed against external interventions. In particular, its goal will be to show that there is a real merging of diagnoses on this subject: a merging that should urge one towards reflection on its causes.

But it seems fundamental to first define what we mean by the phrase "efficiency of an intervention".

The term efficiency is in fact used to allude to different meanings. This clarification is especially necessary when the goal of our examination is not to make a provocative speech but rather to offer a few leads towards improving the real or perceived efficiency of interventions.

1.

Defining Efficiency: A Complicated Mission

Defining the efficiency of a war or an intervention is a difficult exercise. Instead of offering a single definition, it seems wise to take the time to understand the reasons for this complexity. Broadly speaking, let's say that there are three principles we need to keep in mind.

The first is linked to the very nature of war. It's useless to try to establish an exhaustive classification of wars. After Clausewitz, it's enough to consider that between a war of extermination, where one fights for the existence of a nation and a war where "one obeys the disagreeable demands of an alliance brought to an end by force or because it is obsolete"[1], there exist countless wars that take on varying degrees of importance. We can call them "conflict", "intervention" or "engagement", depending on their intensity and the importance we wish to give them. Before talking about efficiency, we must fully grasp the idea that each war

1. Carl von Clausewitz, *De la guerre* (Éditions de Minuit, 1955)

assumes a different level of importance. When France intervened in Afghanistan, even though 88 of its soldiers died there, as shocking as it might seem, it's clear that this was a war of limited interest, since France's vital interests were in no way threatened. Similarly, France is today intervening in the Sahel to "fight terrorism"; is it ready to accept a large number of losses and to sacrifice a portion of its growth in order to attain its objectives? The answer is a resounding no. The French ambition in the Sahel is thus real but limited (limitations seen notably in the use of weapons). This mean that we can't speak in the same way about the efficiency of total war, where a nation is ready to do anything to survive, and the efficiency of limited war, where the effects produced should correspond to a lower level of ambition. In the first case, efficiency would be synonymous with "victory", since the success of the war is linked to the defeat of enemy forces. In the second case, it's not enough to speak of victory: the success of the intervention lies in something other than the mere use of force. In fact, in current engagements, which usually take place in the heart of populations, the notion of victory has lost its meaning: firstly because the adversary commits rarely, or in any case, not for long enough, the error of opposing head-on a western army that forms the front lines or the pocket of a resistance; next, since the difference in force prevents the claiming of a victory, for fear of seeming pretentious or ridiculous. More specifically, army confrontations represent only one of the variables in a much larger equation. This means that today, efficiency is no longer necessarily synonymous with victory. Nonetheless, efficiency remains a reality that we must look into.

The second principle that makes it difficult to define the efficiency of an intervention is linked to the abundance of actors involved. If in the Central African Republic, you were to ask a resident of Bangui, a journalist for *Jeune Afrique*, a French soldier, a Central African politician, a member of the African Union or a UN representative about the effectiveness of Operation Sangaris, you'll probably get as many opinions as there are individuals. The perspectives and expectations of each person will be different, so it's normal for there to no consensus among their definitions, even if certain key elements remain the same. We could make the legitimate objection that in light of history, nothing has changed: different actors in a conflict always have different views. What is new however is the immediacy with which these different actors can communicate and object to ongoing actions; it's the sounding board that is the media; it's the fact that no legitimacy is now necessary in order to impose oneself in a debate. One image, whether an illustration of reality or a manipulation, can immediately influence public opinion and lead to a reorienting of the politics being carried out. We must never lose sight of the perspective from which we consider the study of efficiency.

The third principle that we'd like to mention is that the uncertain character of this work, as we provide definitions, lies in the difficulty of measuring the efficiency of something as difficult to quantify as a military intervention. In the same way that it's difficult to evaluate the economic impact on tourism and construction when organizing a sporting event, it's hard to decide what was caused by a military intervention and what was caused by other factors. It can be very tempting, nonetheless, to try to "objectify" the results produced from external interventions. This means creating an evaluation grid or a system of metrics (an American term now used in French as well): these metrics allow us to compare the situation before, during and after the intervention. Incidentally, one of the symptoms of this western fever to prove efficiency lies in its difficulty to define these criteria, despite their widespread usage. Theoretically, these criteria aim to evaluate the progress of the operation in question. Faced with the impossibility of basing criteria on the attaining of political objectives, they are generally connected with the tactical aspects of implementing counterinsurgency military principles: number of enemy dead and wounded, number of skirmishes, number of civil-military operations completed, etc. The military, assessor of its efficiency, while using its own criteria! This very NATO approach, which disconnects military action from its political objective, does not seem relevant. How does one evaluate the support of the population for Islamist preaching or heir hostility towards an intervening country? How does one measure the stability of a country? How can one determine if the neutralizing of this or that tactically high-value target disrupts a group or if it enables the emergence of a leader who is even more charismatic and competent? It seems that assessing the efficiency of a military intervention is far from being categorical or definitive.

Before we define a few key notions which will allow us to more deeply analyze the essence of efficiency, we should mention the work of British strategist, Liddel Hart, whose work offers an approach that is seductive in its simplicity. In *Strategy*, he explains that a war (and by extension, an intervention) takes on a certain efficiency if the *post*-intervention situation is better than the *pre*-situation. Liddel Hart takes major wars as his examples but this definition can be applied to current military interventions as well. This way of evaluating the efficiency of a conflict has the benefit of connecting efficiency with time and then linking these to the notion of a higher good that can be achieved. Indeed, it's only with time that we can judge the fruits of an intervention. Liddell Hart reminds us that "the goal of war is peace" and that attained military successes should be evaluated using this measuring stick. If, for example, we compare Libya before the intervention of 2011 to Libya today, our assessment would be clear: the intervention has been entirely inefficient or, more precisely, it was efficiently led from a military point of view but it was strategically and politically inefficient. There was no credible[2]

2. More specifically, the National Transitional Council (NTC) declined different "customer service" proposals that were offered; this demonstrates the difficulty of reconciling respect for local sovereignty with the need to pursue destabilizing activities after an initial intervention.

alternative military solution offered to Libyans after the death of Muammar Gaddafi and the country sank into a chaos that helped destabilize the Maghreb and the Sahel but also Europe, as we saw with the development of armed groups and the growing waves of migrants. This kind of reasoning in the long-term is equally interesting when it involves studying the relevance of an intervention. This is, incidentally, what Dominique de Villepin meant when he addressed the United Nations Security Council on February 15, 2003. Opposed to the idea of armed intervention in Iraq, he explained that the situation created by armed engagement would be, given the complexity and volatility of the Middle East, necessarily less good than the situation that existed then. However, Liddell Hart's definition is insufficient when we see how it clashes with the difficulty of its evaluation. How much time do we have to let pass before we can be sure that we have the required space to evaluate the efficiency of an intervention? It seems clear that we need a frame of reference for this notion that will allow us to effectively evaluate efficiency so that, ultimately, we can move forward in this area.

The Three Levels of Efficiency in an Intervention

As we begin our analysis, we will start by emphasizing the three decision-making levels of an intervention: political, strategic and military. These are the levels that we see regularly in strategic literature and that we will try to define through the lens of efficiency.

Firstly, political efficiency falls under the appraisal of the highest state levels as it evaluates national interests. An intervention could be considered politically efficient if the interests of France are guaranteed, if its image is magnified, if its sphere of influence is confirmed or expanded, if it establishes or reinforces its alliances, or if it maintains its position amongst its peers. In this way, political efficiency evaluates less the reality of the executed actions than how they're perceived: what are the consequences of the perception of this intervention for the state and for the executive branch of government? In this capacity, political efficiency also takes into account more party-related interests: this is especially true in a country as centralized or even as "royalist" as France, where the president can decide, alone, to carry out a military intervention. Inevitably, the political leader in charge of the final decision to launch a military operation will take into account domestic policy issues. This, of course, is another constraint to take into account in the stages leading up to implementation; nonetheless, it would be naïve to see here a tilting of institutions. The influence of what Tocqueville called "internal affairs »[3] on "external affairs" is the same in any democracy. It would be naïve to lament it and dangerous to ignore it. Political power is, first and foremost, the only judge of

3. Alexis de Tocqueville, *De la démocratie en Amérique* (Gallimard, 1850)

political efficiency in an intervention. The aims of war are therefore not necessarily communicated or in any case, not all of them are. However, a politico-military dialogue is necessary from this moment forward to help political power determine what is attainable but also for the army to adapt the intensity of its operation in accordance with considered political issues. If political power wants an intervention mainly for a show of power, the military efficiency might, paradoxically, ruin the effect. In a democratic regime, the level of political ambition linked to the management of a limited war must always be in keeping with the image that the executive government creates for itself with the expectations of public opinion. If this is not the case, election results will punish the president who must not have understood the expectations of their electoral base. In this scenario, the image of the intervention that was built and delivered by the media assumes a capital importance since it's a determining factor in deciding public opinion. For these reasons also, a communication strategy, led from the highest state level, is necessary to explain the reasons behind an intervention and have its principles be accepted by its own national population, as well as by the international scene.

Strategic efficiency can be evaluated in the medium or long term. An intervention will be considered strategically efficient if it brings sustainable improvement to a local situation. We might consider regained stability in a country after a vicious cycle of state dereliction, the sustainable neutralizing of threats, the resumption of a peaceful social life or economic activity, a situation of peace with a neighboring country or, at minimum, the return to an acceptable status quo, just as much the criteria that confirm the strategic efficiency of an intervention. We might think that these criteria will lead, more often than not, to political success, meaning the reinforcement, on the international scene, of the position of the intervening country. Strategic efficiency is thus under the responsibility of the main ministries involved, particularly the Ministry of the Armed Forces and the Ministry of Foreign Affairs. The Chief of the General Staff of the Armies occupies a leading role as the head of operations and as the figure, due to his experience, most likely to evaluate the consequences of the use of force on the field. Strategic efficiency is not, therefore, synonymous with victory; in the Central African Republic, for example, a precarious stability that lasts a few years is, without a doubt, a kind of strategic success.

On the ground, military efficiency is the main responsibility of the military itself, even if the construction of the "military tool" depends on political commitment to build it correctly in the long-term. An intervention can be qualified as militarily efficient if the use of force, intelligently organized in the time and space, allows for the obtaining of tactical successes which also contribute to the attainment of strategic and political objectives. As such, it seems that military efficiency cannot be evaluated independently of the objective it serves. The speeches that recognize the military efficiency of an intervention, while simultaneously noting how it didn't allow for strategic or political success demonstrate a demeaning condescension: it implies that military efficiency must perpetually adapt, in terms of its intensity and its modes of action, to the political objective. The idea is that a military success that does not permit the attaining of political success is in reality, a failure.

These three levels of efficiency are intimately linked; they are, however, also organized into a hierarchy. The efficiency of an "lower" level can be evaluated using the criteria of a higher level and cannot enter conflict with it. A military action can have immediate consequences for the strategic level, and for the political level. The chain of command from the political level to the ground level should ensure the coherence of these three levels of efficiency; this coherence, made possible through the joint efforts of the military and diplomatic, are the best way to guarantee the success of an intervention.

In order to not get stuck in theory and make our definition more operational, we will retain seven factors that decisively contribute to the efficiency of an intervention:

- the formulation of clear and attainable political objectives;
- the execution of an interdepartmental strategy;
- the translation of political objectives into military objectives that are attainable by armed forces;
- the provision of sufficient means;
- the building of alliances;

– the support of the population;

– the perception of legitimacy of the operation.

At the end of this work of defining, it's clear that there are many elements that could prevent the fulfillment of these criteria. The goals of war will always be blurry, interdepartmental work will always be complicated, attainable military objectives will be formulated with difficulty, means will always be carefully watched over, legitimacy and international support will never be definitively acquired... The goal of our essay, after this detour into theory, is to provide a cool analysis of how things really are, in order to understand why it's so hard for us to create the conditions for full efficiency.

2.

The Inefficiency Felt by Interested Parties

At the political level

Two different areas can be distinguished within the political level : that of the executive who decides on the intervention and assumes responsibility for it and that of the political world in a larger sense, including parliamentarians, but also political parties who have opinions to defend regarding the intervention, opinions that concern its justification as well as its execution. Each country naturally possesses its own democratic tradition, going from a total empowerment of Parliament to a kind of "hyper-presidency". In the case of France, the functioning of institutions reinforces the President's status of Commander-in-Chief. The decision to parachute into Kolwezi is attributed to Valéry Giscard d'Estaing while Jacques Chirac is considered responsible for the decision to not intervene in Iraq in 2003; Nicolas Sarkozy decided to intervene in Libya and François Hollande to intervene in Mali. Presidents are made into heroes, emerge as warlords, a status even reinforced in the Fifth Republic with its possession of nuclear weapons. This pride felt by French presidents, as they assume the role of Commander-in-Chief is evident during their presidential terms. Each is tempted to maintain the sovereignty of the country and to present to his people a brilliant epic, often exotic, that cuts through the gloominess of the news on weakening growth or the rise in unemployment. The images of President Hollande in Timbuktu or of President Sarkozy in Benghazi immediately come to mind. But the overall situation is similar in states where the decision to send troops is a parliamentary one; take the example of Tony Blair's military mingling with the crowds in Basra. The United States is no exception to this rule: recall President Bush announcing, in May 2003, "major combat operations have ended" while on board the aircraft carrier, USS Abraham Lincoln.

While decisions regarding an intervention don't systematically win unanimous support, a certain sacred union seems to prevail, at least at first, reducing to a secondary role the one and only advisory vote of the parliamentarians who weigh in four months after the start of the intervention. The initial phase of the intervention is thus very often a success as is generally the case in asymmetrical warfare where the differences in strength are so great; before understanding that they should opt for a guerrilla warfare strategy, the enemy tries to frontally oppose and quickly pays the price for this decision. The result is a period of a few months, during which time, the feeling of victory prevails, the task force is acclaimed and it seems the Cassandras who delivered warnings were hugely mistaken. We see the classic but always appreciated staging of the parade for the liberators, acclaim from the crowd and speeches, often successful, from western political authorities. Political power naturally takes advantage of the successes gained on the international scene. A boost in popularity in the polls is often the first benefit: what citizenry can remain unmoved as a foreign population raises its national flag and not feel gratitude for its political leaders?

One of the inevitable consequences of this interaction between foreign policy and domestic policy is the temptation of the politician to interfere on the tactical level, or even the tactical-media level to be sure that the rhythm of military operations remains subordinate to the domestic policy agenda, or in any case, coincides with it. This can result in a loss of the long-term vision if the political objective of the mission is slowly replaced by the objectives of individual parties.

After this initial phase, there usually follows a disengagement from politics, one that coincides with a period when the situation on the ground grows increasingly complicated. Media attention dwindles and political pressure on military operations slackens. Nonetheless, armies don't have more freedom of action. In fact, political power becomes very sensitive to all of the elements which, in the hands of the media, could transform an initial success into a "stalemate", or "a neocolonial intervention" or a "recollection of Françafrique [a term referring to France's relationship with its former African colonies]". The question of losses becomes significant: in order to avoid, even on a small scale, the Vietnam "Body Bag" Syndrome, armies are invited to lean towards the "zero death option". This situation, tactically hard to understand while the circumstances deteriorate, has the effect of forcing the military to make difficult choices and clearly limiting their efficiency. A large gap emerges between the military engaged on the ground, seeking out tactical efficiency and the politicians who, disappointed by the weak developments and thus the weak political gains, have the impression that the local situation is escaping them and that the armies are sometimes carrying out their own war, without taking into consideration the political constraints to which they should remain subordinate. As a result, there are regular attempts by politicians to "regain control" over the supposedly overly emancipated military. The case of Afghanistan is particularly interesting. In the spring of 2011, after a series of significant losses on the part of the French military contingent, President Sarkozy wanted to "regain control": there was then an incompatibility between the strategy that had been executed and the new political goal to leave Afghanistan and take no further tactical risks. In another position, after his election in 2009, President Barack Obama wanted to adopt a strategy that looked to avoid stalemate while the conditions for success were no longer present and the military was divided as to the course to follow. This gap between politics and the military expresses itself most notably in the speeches made by politicians who, little by little, distance themselves from reality in order to try to give political meaning to current operations.

In terms of what concerns the political world in a larger sense, and not only the executive portion of it, the evolution it follows is generally similar. After a phase of support for the intervention and an analysis of the political gains in favor of the executive branch and of the president in particular, the parliamentarians and leaders of the different parties slowly begin to voice criticisms regarding the legitimacy of the operation and the manner in which it is being conducted. They will first do it to take advantage of the feeling of stalemate maintained by media outlets and will seem like enlightened opponents to the executive branch, which they will depict as warmongers and free with the lives of soldiers. They will next justify their parliamentarian role, especially in France, where they will underline in front of their voters that they have not been willing parties in this decision[1].

In the end, it seems that the same pattern repeats itself across different modes. After an initial phase where the military and politics seem to work together,

---

1. Senate report no. 794. Information report completed in the name of the Committee on Foreign Affairs, the Defense Committee and the Armed Services Committee, to assess external operations. Authors: Messrs. Jacques Gautier, Daniel Reiner, Jean-Marie-Bockel, Jeanny Lorgeoux, Cédric Perrin and Gilbert Roger.

a distance is gradually created. Politicians are surprised, after a promising beginning, at the overall inefficiency of the interventions in terms of both operational and political gains: they will therefore look to regain control but will note their limited room for maneuver. They will feel trapped by the military approach, which they understand poorly, and will ultimately feel distrustful of the armies. In the end, for politicians, the repetition of interventions and the global assessment of recent major operation do not argue in favor of the efficiency of the proposed military solutions[2].

Inefficiency in the Eyes of the Population and Public Opinion

The population's feelings about interventions are intimately linked to the politicians over which they exert such influence. The population isn't, generally speaking, hostile towards warlike presidents and accepts easily enough the arguments presented by the executive branch in favor or not of an intervention. Whether we're talking about the 1991 intervention in Iraq, the engagement in Afghanistan after September 11, 2001, the refusal to intervene in Iraq in 2003 or the interventions in Libya

2. Senate report no. 794, July 2016. Information report completed in the name of the Committee on Foreign Affairs, the Defense Committee and the Armed Services Committee, to assess external operations. Authors: Messrs. Jacques Gautier, Daniel Reiner, Jean-Marie-Bockel, Jeanny Lorgeoux, Cédric Perrin and Gilbert Roger.

in 2011 and Mali in 2012, on each of these occasions, the population mostly went along with the reasons that were cited. Even if there wasn't a consensus, the population didn't see interventions as something to get worked up about. The initial successes of the interventions, which were generally translated into beautiful images of equipment, short interviews with motivated soldiers and lovely landscapes, aroused the support of the population. Additionally, the moral values espoused by these operations inspired pride, as did the assumed values of courage, effort and camaraderie, and the elevation of the universal and humanist values to which the western world is so attached, especially when brought up by the "liberated peoples" themselves!

In any case, public opinion comes from a population that we could describe as being both lazy and discerning. Lazy because it gets bored fast; not having delved into the details or the initial reasons for the intervention, nor the military and local political issues, it's not looking to understand why the pace has slowed or the difficulties encountered. Current media outlets, which like to bounce back and forth between subjects, are of little help with this. However, public opinion is also very discerning. Even if it feels unconcerned by the initial decisions leading up to an intervention, it very correctly sees the personal political benefits that the executive government can reap from it. In particularly, it astutely recognizes the duplicity of certain arguments that attempt to justify the slowness of operations or mask the true objectives of an intervention. It cannot be fooled, not by romanticized, idealistic speeches, such as when an NGO tries to highlight the personal thriving of local populations, and not by alarmist speeches that use uncertain shortcuts to explain that the quiet at the Saint-Michel subway stop is directly linked to these distant interventions.

The recent apologies from Tony Blair, the "regrets" about the 2003 intervention expressed by Colin Powell, or even the accusations made against Nicolas Sarkozy and his connections with Muammar Gaddafi could put a dent in the public's trust in the political motivations behind interventions.

Broadly speaking, the population has trouble understanding the slowness of operations, why operations have to be maintained over long periods of time or why their end isn't considered in terms of reaching a tangible objective. We could say that public opinion, just like the political world, is stuck on a very classic blueprint of war: a succession of battles until a single decisive battle, the destruction of the enemy's center allowing for the signing of a treaty and the return of the troops. Nonetheless, this blueprint of war seems well and truly over in the context of today's long conflicts. This critical feeling towards the efficiency of interventions doesn't, in any case, detract from the population's attachment to the armed forces nor its belief in their professionalism. Information report no. 794 from the Senate underlines this situation. "Public opinion, seeing the results as underwhelming, fragile and never definitively gained, despite the very heavy price that is sometimes paid, feels a kind of weariness that we might call "war fatigue". [...] Already, the debate takes on new perspectives: is military success enough to "win the peace", should France focus solely on this element in order to get the effect she seeks?" We could even go so far as to say that public opinion has a political consciousness when it comes to the issues surrounding military operations and this awareness should not be underestimated. Let us recall, for example, that the number of people killed in former Yugoslavia was higher than in Afghanistan but the population was not especially moved because it understood that this engagement held important stakes for Europe itself.

Inefficiency in the Eyes of the Military

While the top brass of the military, whose vision of the system as a whole is aided by its proximity to politicians, remains cautious when faced with the possibility of an intervention, the forces first experience enthusiasm when it comes to interventions: what better way to prove their usefulness than to actually use them! They also have a culture of projection that materializes during these interventions. The obligations and the warnings, the training, the purchased materials, the recruited and trained soldiers: all of these efforts are now justified! The army also believes that it possesses an ancient expertise in task force operations which, although not vital to the survival of the country, remain no less regular and directly linked to their rank and ambition. France, in particular, since the time of Napoleon III, has developed and maintained a true expertise. These interventions awaken in the armed forces memories of reading works by their Elders: Maréchal Lyautey's theories on fighting rebellions, Gallieni's "oil spot method", books on the wars of colonization and decolonization, the counterinsurgency theories of Trinquier and Gallula, responses to experiences on different military engagements in Africa. In short, the mental blueprints are in place, although there is also a general forgetting that for most of the examples cited, the military authority which was responsible for the intervention had both civil and military power: Maréchal Lyautey was Resident-General when he was in Morocco and General de Lattre was High Commissioner when he arrived in Indochina.

The result is an initial period, when the armies are, in general, very effective, since the military objectives are in perfect harmony with the political ends. During this phase, military efficiency can fully express itself, without too many political considerations to block the action. Armies can demonstrate the full extent of their operational abilities, in very different environments: the mountains of Afghanistan, the third quarter of Libya, the Sahel's deserts or the tropics of the Central African Republic.

Frustrations emerge during the phase called "stabilization", which follows intervention. Troops have trouble going from coercion to reconstruction or support. This is exacerbated by the fact that this theoretical passage from one phase to the next often coincides with growing complexity on the ground. After the initial status of liberator comes that of "occupying force"; the enemy which, up until then, was surprised by the pace and capacities of the West has adapted itself by immersing itself in the cities and initiating guerrilla warfare, in which it excels; local partners who are supposed to be gradually taking on the responsibility of local security are lacking. In short, little by little, forces lose the initiative, despite a surplus of effort and imagination. The military therefore refocuses on counterinsurgency methods, which it applies only partially, given the constraints imposed upon it. More precisely, in looking to reconcile the constraints that are more party-related than political with the often contradictory military priorities, the counterinsurgency approach will be misrepresented and thus will lose its efficiency. The military knows it should immerse itself in the populations' environments but to protect itself, it will build FOBs[3] in which it will take refuge and limit its contact to exchanges with local leaders; it knows that it should travel around the area but it will do so with such heavy equipment that it will lose any element of surprise and will have so few troops that it won't be visible; it knows that it should earn and impose respect but in order to avoid any risk, it will use means that are so disproportionate that it will lose its credibility in the eyes of

3. *Forward Operating Base* (FOB): the American term for their army camps

its opponents, as well as the population. The balance between political ends and military objectives, means and approaches is lost, and with it goes the feeling of efficiency.

As a result, a certain fatalism takes hold of the military, as it reflects on the meaning of its mission and the efficiency of what it has accomplished. It's well aware that not all bearers of weapons are necessarily an enemy but, without a political project of reconstruction to carry out, it's placed in a situation where it's limited to retaliating against those who attack it, without offering any credible alternatives; while doing so, it's aware that it's pushing away a large portion of the forces in attendance. The military is perfectly aware of the complexity of local issues but it can only note equally the weakness of the project that it's executing. What were the possibilities offered to the Afghan populations in terms of governance? What guarantees of safety were given to populations, once coalitions had left? What credible project was proposed to the Tuareg people so that they could trust the French forces? The military feels strongly the fragility of the responses that it can bring to these questions, all the more so because it is regularly asked these by the local population. It feels a great temptation, not to do nothing but to do what it knows best. Since strategic objectives are out of reach given the means at its disposal, the military continues to "carry out operations", much like a musician who continues to play his score, not understanding that the rest of the orchestra has stopped playing...A perfect example of the cynicism that can surreptitiously take hold can be seen in this excerpt from La guerre moderne, written in 1961 by Colonel Trinquier[4] and still relevant today: "In the end, the guarantee of never running the risk of a clear defeat that the field or an opponent might inflict upon us allows any military leader to command operations. If the enemies aren't destroyed, at least the geographical objectives were attained in the expected period of time; a few killed rebels will always sound good in a written report. If a few weapons could be recovered, the operation which usually assumes the appearance of a peacetime maneuver then takes on the air of victory and is a sufficient flash to satisfy less demanding leadership."

The feeling of fatalism experienced by soldiers can even evolve into a feeling of defiance towards political authorities. In fact, as Poirier reminds us in Stratégie intégrale et guerre limitée, "for the soldier, limited war does not exist!". When political power imposes more and more limitations on the military to restrict the war to the level of ambition that it has fixed for itself, especially in accordance with its perception of the expectations of public opinion, it limits the action of the military machine, at the precise moment when, following its natural inclination for efficiency, this last takes all the trouble in the world to take back the initiative! The French intervention in Afghanistan in 2011 and 2012 is the perfect example of these moments

4. Colonel Roger Trinquier, *La guerre moderne* (Economica, 2008)

when military efficiency tends to clash with political ambition. During this time, marked by the repeated deaths of soldiers in Afghanistan, public opinion was clear about its weariness in the face of an engagement that it no longer understood. During the summer of 2011, President Sarkozy, thinking about re-election, had inevitably revised downwards the ambition of the engagement in Afghanistan; the only imperative was to avoid losses, at all costs. The military machine engaged in the Afghan valleys, grappling with an opponent grew more aggressive, saw its freedom of maneuver greatly reduced. The soldiers felt obliged to not leave their small forts, except when they had to get more supplies. As the main beneficiaries of this restriction of military efficiency, the Taliban regained their freedom of maneuver, got back the upper hand over the population and increased the pressure on French forces. Our goal here is not to incriminate political authority, which acted according to the rules of the game, as set by our democracies. The objective is simply to show that inefficiency, both real and felt, comes from an incoherence between political ends, military goals, strategies and means. A number of officers understand this analysis well. On the other hand, we cannot ask our young soldiers, in whom we stoke the fires of audacity and fearlessness, to understand this. In situations where there's a lack of understanding, which can become unbearable as the blood keeps flowing and the lack of ambition is felt, only military discipline and allegiance to the leader guarantees loyalty to the military machine.

Inefficiency Felt by Countries Acting as Sites of Intervention

"Thank you France!" Before being put into question or criticized, external interventions are more often than not welcomed with enthusiasm since they mean, in the vast majority of cases, avoiding great danger: massacre, the fall of a capital, civil war... During these intense moments of communion between two peoples that the colonial adventure has marked, political authorities usually prefer to fully live these historical moments, making great use of bombastic speeches, forgetting that a strategic victory can only be evaluated in the long-term.

Unfortunately, this state of grace never lasts very long. The time of small French flags on the edges of paths seems quickly forgotten, leaving room for dull incomprehension. And so, the syndrome of "occupation troops" is gently put into place. The image of an ecosystem may allow us to better understand this reality. A military intervention, even if it takes all the precautions in the world, is a kick to these "ecosystems" that we're describing. This kick can be taken well, or at least understood, when the previous ecosystem has become unlivable. But very quickly, populations, almost instinctively, are in search of a new order that will allow them to live and thrive. Very naturally, they turn towards the intervening power and expect it to establish the new order that it has come to launch. Unfortunately, these populations quickly realize that the proposed, let's call it "political project", is neither credible nor even desirable. To the question: "does the survival of my family depend on my support of the NATO project in Afghanistan", there are few Afghans who would have responded positively. When we directly asked this question of some Afghans, who enjoyed nothing more than sweeping discussions about geopolitics, they responded: "In three, four or ten years, you will be gone. The only ones left will be us and the Taliban..." In the same way, there are many Africans who mock our attitude; they see us as strong, armed and protected from head to toe, swearing our unconditional support to the powers in place, but also not hesitating to use violence as soon as it involves re-establishing public order. Eventually, populations accuse us of not understanding what Africa is: a land where local, tribal and familial governance is strong; a land where violence is still a way to settle widespread conflicts; a land, in the end, where the principles of liberal democracy cannot be transposed without first being adapted.

Of course, populations see the redoubled efforts of the military to "conquer hearts and minds" and to improve their daily lives: digging wells, reopening schools, distributing blankets, providing care for people and their livestock, bringing electricity to remote areas, financing roads, etc. Everything is attempted to try to restore the trust between intervening forces and populations. The building of mosques has even been financed by American taxpayers, in an attempt to convince Pashtuns from the Kunar province in Afghanistan that the coalition is there for them and respects the country's "Muslim integrity". Even without referring to the local lack of, it would still be perfectly untrue to claim that these actions manage to attain what should be the goal of a force that is intervening at the core of a population: making the inhabitants of the intervention zone understand that the "political project" supported by forces is the only one among all competing offers (Taliban, Islamic State, etc.) to guarantee the survival of social entities (families, tribes, countries, nations).

As we end this analysis of local populations' perception of external interventions, we must not omit the irrationality which quickly resurfaces when incomprehension settles in. "If France makes so many sacrifices while also not caring about the security of native populations, shouldn't there be a reason for that?" It becomes extremely complicated to explain that "no", we did not have secret intelligence that the ground in northern Mali and northern Niger were overflowing with oil and gold. Along the same lines, the years of Françafrique makes the myth that France wants to divide in order to rule last even longer when to the contrary, we dream of only one thing: uniting in order to leave under improved circumstances.

The notion of an intervention's efficiency therefore seems extremely relative and cannot be understood unless we specifying the point of view from which we consider the question and the kind of intervention that we'd like to study. One thing is sure: today, efficiency is no longer synonymous with victory, and while it's sometimes necessary, it's far from being enough.

*

Despite the relative character of efficiency, there is a constant that emerges: efficiency is best when there's coherence between the effects produced by the military machine and the expectations of the executive government, one that is made possible through a fair allotment of means and the operating strategies that are chosen. Unfortunately, this initial coherence withers most often with time, the seeking of military efficiency clashing with differing political imperatives. From this situation comes a feeling of incomprehension, even reciprocal defiance, between soldiers bitterly regretting what they perceive as being a lack of ambition and a political world that has come to doubt the very relevance of interventions, as points out a Parliament report[5]: "A review of on external operations carried out by France in the last fifty years yields mixed results. The military assessment is very positive. [...] The political assessment of French external operations is clearly more nuanced. The complicated futures of the operations launched left and right during the years 1990 and 2000 cause doubts about the efficiency of the military tool when used in response to external crises." What to do when faced with this fatality, which tends to constrict our operations in what General Bentégeat calls the cycle of "emotion-intervention-weariness-retreat"? Many attitudes are possible.

5. Parliamentary report no. 2777, May 2016

The first consists of, for the military, to not reconsider their way of intervening, since "the military assessment is very positive". In a way, this means deciding that armed forces are fulfilling their part of the contract and that it's up to other departments and the executive government to take their share of responsibility.

A second, more constructive, attitude says that the armed forces are not only responsible for military efficiency; their role is not limited to making their weapons efficiently do the talking during "kinetic" phases. Armies are also "co-responsible" for strategic efficiency. To this end, since the paradigms that have been inherent to our interventions in these last years are not translatable into clear successes, it's important to question their relevance. That means that the objective from now on is to determine to what extent the inefficiency regularly highlighted in current interventions is attributable to an unsuitability within our strategies and approaches.

The Limits of Current Strategies

Faced with the lack of long-term stability efficiency in external operations, a number of voices are making themselves heard as they offer ideas for changes in concepts, organization and capacity, which would allow for improvement in the efficiency of future engagements. What are these voices? Firstly, there are those in charge of the executive government. Since they must ceaselessly prove to voters the relevance of their choices in regards to safety, voters who are simultaneously worried about the terrorist threat and skeptical about distant wars, the executive government must deploy all its talent to give, with instruction, a meaning to their choices. There are next the experts of the strategic community who, after having characterized the new forms of conflicts (often by designating them with new adjectives), risk a few conjectures about the future. And finally, there are the journalists and the public commentators, who, with more or less talent, use airtime and newspaper columns to air out big thought patterns that, in their eyes, illuminate the world we know and provide the keys to counter threats.

It is unthinkable to make an exhaustive list of all the ideas emerging today about how to improve the efficiency of our military interventions. However, it is still possible to highlight a few larger trends and main ideas that regularly turn up in public debate. The second part of our analysis will thus try to present these ideas that energize the strategic community. Far from simply describing them, we will show what relevance these reflections might have and to what problems they're trying to bring solutions. We will also emphasize that in most cases, these tracks of thinking are not directly contributing to restoring the efficiency of military interventions: if they seem, upon first impression, to possess an element of truth, they will not allow for the attaining of fixed objectives and generally speaking, only establish mantras. In short, our concern in this part is not to showcase the intellectual defeat of the strategic community but rather, to demonstrate that good diagnoses are associated with solutions that either need improvement or are faulty and old myths have been replaced with new myths, that while more in keeping with the evolution of our vision of the world, remain far from the pragmatism required to examine the management of efficient military interventions.

I.

The Dead-Ends of the Comprehensive Approach

The comprehensive approach is a recent concept that has known great success, so much so that today, it's universally employed in western countries. The term began to appear in the nineties, as the world started to adapt itself to the conflicts emerging after the Cold War. The appearance of more limited conflicts and the new role of populations among whose ranks armies intervene have given rise to a new strategy that emphasizes the need for civilian-military coordination, in order to reach strategic objectives. Today, this term is constantly used, on the national level and within coalitions or large organizations like NATO, the EU and the UN. It has gradually almost become a dogma: its conceptual simplicity, with the lack of exact or shared definitions, greatly favoring its propagation. The comprehensive approach, which is almost impossible to define, given how many different nations and institutions have different visions of it, relies on the idea that to "win peace", we must carry out coordinated actions following the triptych of security-governance-development. Within this framework, a number of important actors must be able to coordinate amongst themselves to, in each of their areas of expertise, contribute to the attaining of a final goal. This involves a single approach and isn't uniquely a military strategy because it can be seen from the highest level of the state (interdepartmental level) and organizations to the tactical level, where individual units are deployed on the field. It is presented as a response to the growing complexity of international interventions and based on the idea that the origin of contemporary crises lies, before all, on the decay of states, not their hostility. The comprehensive approach allows its supporters to fit interventions into the philosophy of an era that is distrustful of operations and is in fact eager to enjoy "the dividends of peace": the comprehensive approach thus insists on the fact that "the solution is not only military", that balance is necessary, that coordination with non-military actors is crucial...

This excerpt from an opinion piece written by General de Villiers, formerly Chief of the General Staff of the Armies (Chef d'État-Major des Armées or CEMA) which was published in Le Monde on January 20, 2016 provides a good definition of the mindset behind this approach: "A strategy based only on military effects [...] will never be able to act on the roots of violence, when these are anchored in the lack of hope, education, justice, development, governance and respect. Winning the war isn't enough to win the peace. No matter the natures of the crises, a comprehensive approach—meaning an interdepartmental and international approach—is indispensable. This requires time and there is no place for development—economic, but also sustainable—without security, just as there is no security without development." Described in this way, this vision seems grounded in common sense and difficult to criticize.

And yet, this approach and the manner in which it is understood and applied, is inevitably the fruit of an era; it is the bearer of an ideological backdrop that makes it structurally, barely qualified to face current issues. When we look at how it is implemented today, the comprehensive approach establishes an impasse. Nonetheless, it remains a vision to which political and military authorities cling. Even if it has been regularly appealed to for the last fifteen years, there exist only a few examples where its use has proved to be successful; no method has concretely established the way in which this approach could be understood effectively on the field. We can certainly point to the difficulty of local situations to explain the challenge of testing it; we can also consider that the inability to use this approach can be explained by the ideology that underlies it and by the vagueness of its definition. Its high-level design, much like its concrete implementation, suffers from its character of being barely operational. In looking to address all of the aspects of the crisis, simultaneously, it acknowledges the complexity without going so far as to rationalize it. This situation ends by pushing those on the ground to a certain resignation. Since it's "complex", since the responsibilities are watered down, they end up convincing themselves that the responsibility for the slowness or the noted lack of success falls to other pillars of the comprehensive approach and that therefore, "it will take years" to reap the benefits of the efforts being made today. The complexity thus justifies the great length of time and ends by validating the idea that success on the ground is impossible. It also justifies certain excesses that, as it happens, we can observe on the ground: extensive misuse of development aid, a blind belief in the capacities of local forces to take charge of the sovereignty of their states, the misguided use of force. For the military, the comprehensive approach has become an unattainable political fiction, even though it is, in fact, considered to be the main responsible party for its implementation. The main "fog of war" has now changed in nature. It is less linked to the will of the enemy or the feasibility of the field, as it was in the time of Clausewitz. It is, in part, created by our concerns and finds its source in the incoherence of the implementation of the comprehensive approach. We will develop here its three main limits.

The first limit is a conceptual one. The comprehensive approach, far from only involving the coherence of the civil and military dimensions of an intervention, is a true groundswell which looks to deeply transform the institutional, economic and social situation of a country. It's a significant act of intrusion since it involves, in a way, the changing of the DNA of a country all while defending it. The usual conversation that has developed at the same time about the supposed respect of the sovereignty of local actors is thus barely credible for those actors. For that matter, it's hardly astonishing that this concept has been developed at the moment when the messianic vision of western interventions has also triumphed. This violence is especially felt by the local actors of the host countries; if they directly admit and tolerate that a foreign country intervene in certain cases on their soil, in order to solve a security problem, in accordance with their interests, the comprehensive approach is lived through as a humiliation; what is especially upsetting for local populations is that widespread poverty has led authorities to feign their support, in order to make sure that they receive anticipated subsidies. The comprehensive approach inevitably seems like the corollary to state building, a strategic vision so well accepted that it's generally preceded by a description of the country which will be the object of the intervention as being a "failed state", a vague term that's especially handy to screen western motivations behind humanist virtues. The State having "failed", the intervening countries consider that it should not only serve their own interests but that it's legitimate to try to fill the void left in security, governance and development. It's to this end that western armies look to recreate or form local armies according to their own standards, to lead development activities without necessarily adapting them to local hierarchies and norms, to promote modes of governance that are undoubtedly relevant from an intellectual point of view but which are ill-adapted in the local context. However, the expression "failed state" is "deceptive in that it puts the emphasis on a process of disintegration when what usually prevails is an old absence. [...] There where for a few decades it has been possible to create the illusion of a state in fits and starts of civil and military cooperation, the economic difficulties [...] have quickly revealed that it was a question of straw buildings."[1] The blurring around the term "failed state" tends to hide the fact that the countries in which we intervene are very often "non-states". In a way, if this meant merely filling a void or restoring a previously existing order, by creating an administration, security forces and schools, the situation would be relatively simple. But the absence of the state and the political deficit have for a long time been filled by other infra-state actors like militias, tribal solidarities, mafia networks or questionable NGOs that are sponsored by the Gulf countries, thus allowing for the proliferation of radical Islam. "The war is becoming the main fabric of society, the national construction. The war is producing an economy that is helping a lot of the actors thrive; the war is also becoming a space of mobilization, identification but worse still, the war is becoming a kind of social protection. One whole part of the population [...] finds in the war the means to exist and to be socially protected."[2] In this context, the comprehensive approach is an illusion because the

1. Dominique de Villepin, *op. cit.*
2. Bertrand Badie and Dominique Vidal, Nouvelles guerre : comprendre les conflits du XXIe siècle (La Découverte, 2016)

intervening countries have neither the means nor the ambition to create, or recreate, out of nothing, a viable state, whether "means" here refers to people, money, time or energy. In the end, the comprehensive approach will waver between two options: either the completion of high-visibility projects, extremely ambitious and costly that will clash with the states' inabilities to structure them, make a success of them and protect them from corruption; or the achieving of cosmetic changes, done in different areas, in order to have the force accepted and the collateral damage pardoned, to give the illusion of progress in order to justify an imminent withdrawal or to communicate more easily on the positive effects of the intervention.

The second limit is of an organizational sort; it involves the difficulty of coordinating the myriad actors necessary for the implementation of a comprehensive approach. Since the approach is "comprehensive", all of the actors, meaning all of the ministries, are therefore, in theory, concerned. It is artificially possible to gather them together into three distinct groups: security actors (armies, intelligence services), governance and civil cooperation actors (diplomatic services, consulting firms) and development actors (investment funds, NGOs). Without going into all of the details of the specific features of each of these entities, it's quickly obvious that these different actors are very different in terms of their objectives, their functions and their visions of the world. Worse still, suspicion can prevail between these entities. In the absence of a clear hierarchy, each has a tendency to caricature the other to justify its refusal to work together: the military as a warmonger without vision, the diplomat as a smooth talker who refuses to adapt his generous ideas to real life and the development agencies as being more concerned about their independence from the first two than about the progress being made. In these conditions, the need for interdepartmental and interagency coordination is known but difficult to attain. It is, for example, expressed in these terms in the official report (Livre blanc) of 2013: "The consolidation of fragile states or the reestablishment of their stability requires the implementation of a group of complementary and coherent actions in all areas. An increased coordination is necessary within the framework of an interdepartmental and multilateral global approach, in order to optimize the use of the means taken into consideration." And yet, this need for coordination, which is the conclusion of all the analyses regarding our external interventions, does not translate itself into facts. This is especially the case in the analysis of the information report completed in 2016 by the senators in the Defense Committee on the assessment of external operations[3]. They explain that, despite the necessity of to more "effectively organize the French means likely to be engaged abroad within the framework of civilian-military operations", France has not managed to equip itself with an "interdepartmental

3. Parliamentary report no. 2777 from the National Assembly, May 2016

strategy for civilian-military management in external crises". This has been "abandoned in the graveyard of useless administrative production". The senators responsible for the writing of this report have questioned, on this point, the Minister for Foreign Affairs. The response is illuminating: "[...] Piloted by the Ministry of Foreign Affairs (Ministre de l'Europe et des Affaires étrangères or MEAE), the 2009 interdepartmental strategy regarding management of external crises led, in 2010, to the setting up of an interdepartmental task force for civilian-military management of crises, placed under the responsibility of MEAE. The swiftly increasing complexity and numbers of the EO (external operations), as well as important institutional changes on the side of the MEAE, have made it so that the strategy of 2009 and its interdepartmental plan for the management of external crises have gradually decreased in operability. In the absence of a true, single interdepartmental process, defined ahead of time and replicable for each crisis (as was forecast by the 2009 strategy), there exists in the central administration, at this stage in MEAE, more of an ad hoc quality to the interdepartmental coordinations." What can we conclude from this response? Very simply that when faced with the difficulties of the ministries to work together, the need for coordination is first translated into the creation of a task force; a task force which, when faced with the abundance and complexity of the crises is next transformed into a multitude of task forces! This increase in coordination units shows the realty of the preeminence of localized logic systems.

In the absence of a clear chain that would allow for the coordination and subordination of each of the pillars (security, governance, development) in accordance with the situations and efforts supported, the comprehensive approach isn't able to exist. Without the coherence that would come from a single source of piloting from the highest levels, there prevails a logic of different perimeters and schools of thought. Lars Apfel, a German officer, notes in an article in Le Monde from April 24, 2012 that "civil actors, with their irreplaceable skills, who would have gradually replaced the military are so limited that they cannot produce significant effects. Militaries thus find themselves pressured to take on tasks that aren't theirs." After four years of existence, Operation Barkhane, like the organization of G5 Sahel, has not been able to develop and coordinate the pillars of "governance" and "development" in its strategy. Reflections on the operational efficiency should therefore offer a mode of organization that manages to minimize this tendency towards division, while refraining from offering a miracle solution that consists of creating a new task force!

The vagueness felt at the interdepartmental level can be found on the ground as well. The comprehensive approach is seen as a challenge by generals. It's they, in fact, who are the best placed to note the gap between, on one side, the political desire to develop the pillars of governance and development and on the other, the reality of the tactical and security situation which removes all credibility from this project. Caught between a rock and a hard place, the general staff might be tempted to force the hand of destiny a little by adjusting the "security indicators" presented to the political authorities by replacing a little of the red with some green, or with orange on the location maps... Through a subtle Impressionist game, convincing those at the decision-making level that the security situation is "certainly worrying but making progress" isn't very complicated, if one has sufficiently mastered the color charts of PowerPoint software. But the desire to forcefully impose the implementation of this comprehensive approach also leads to blunders in the management of operations. The militaries force themselves to include, in the orders for operations, paragraphs for "development" or "governance" without these really ever justifying themselves. Local populations have a hard time understanding the change in the military's position, which the security situation isn't enough to explain. The military detachments which are present on the ground do not have the civil cooperation tools they need to implement often wise ideas: restore local legal systems, encourage agriculture and animal husbandry, to the detriment of drug trafficking... The concerned French ministries themselves often do not have the structures and the personnel to fulfill this kind of mission. On their side, the military have neither the necessary expertise nor the skill to stand in for them. The militaries present on the ground will therefore have the main responsibility of implementing this comprehensive approach; they will in that case "do their best": they'll use force judiciously and mix a slight humanitarianism into their actions, thinking that they're carrying out development activities when, in reality, they're only leading influence operations to make the force accepted: digging wells, providing supplies of all kinds, organizing visits from veterinarians and doctors. The militaries invoke Gallula, Trinquier and Lyautey to justify the incoherence and the vagueness, while forgetting, as Gallieni underlined, that peace-building activities only make sense once "the submission of the inhabitants has been obtained"; which is far from being the case today. Making the military play, at the same time, the part of a soldier and a humanitarian is rarely effective.

One of the consequences of this incapability to implement this comprehensive approach will be the leaning towards the bureaucratization and excessive enlargement of the general staff. This strategy, which claims to be a uniting force, leads logically enough to the excess of planning and examination of ideas without any sort of order, in an attempt to contain everything, to study all possible hypotheses. It's enough, on this subject, to observe an American member of the general staff in operations, who aligns hundreds of "planners" working on dozens of planning options in order to understand where the comprehensive approach will lead us when it's developed to its maximum. The desire to include all aspects of a situation, without having available the tools to do it efficiently, the gap between political expectations and the reality on the ground, as well as the blurriness of the respective perimeters of the different actors will all lead to a certain inhibition of force; the bureaucracy, the procedures will end by heavily limiting this approach's action. The phenomenon of bureaucratization is such that we associate it today, not without cynicism, with a fighting unit having to complete a weighty PowerPoint presentation, approved by the highest authorities in the military theater, just to get out of a military camp to an external operation abroad, without neglecting to make sure that the authorities in Paris are also kept up to speed. We are far from the autonomy of small tactical levels, one of the criteria that is unanimously recognized as being a necessary condition of success. In a way, only special forces have managed to maintain a relatively low degree of bureaucratization, one that is, in any case, compatible with the reactivity that the management of these operations requires.

This phenomenon of bureaucratization is particularly well-described by Graham Allison in his book, Essence of Decision: Explaining the Cuban Missile Crisis. He explains that in a bureaucratic organization, those in power, when confronted with a problem, do not take it on as a single entity but instead, prefer to break it up into smaller parts, on which distinct organization will work. In the same way, bureaucratic organizations always favor respecting the standardized procedures that reassure them. In the end, these organizations will cling to the plan, as much as they can, even when it is objectively at odds with reality. The comprehensive approach, as we know it today, seems to be a perfect example. As we come to the end of these few lines highlighting the link between bureaucratization and the comprehensive approach, this doesn't mean that we should make the mistake of blaming the comprehensive approach alone for the bureaucratic tendencies of our general staffs. The desire of the executive government to carefully follow operations in real time in order to not have to endure the media tempo, because it imposes a frenzied reporting, is in all likelihood the primary cause of this bureaucratization. The American influence, powerfully exercised via NATO procedures is undeniably the second cause. The centralism of Paris-based general staff members, made possible thanks to the improvement of transmitting systems and made necessary by the political control previously described, represents the third cause. All of these reasons put end-to-end, it becomes possible to understand the overexcitement of general staff members towards troops who grow ever more numerous.

The third limit of the global approach is linked to the relationship with time. The engagement of armed forces in western countries, notably in France, has always been thought of in a chronological way, following an operational trailer called: "the continuum of operations". This continuum describes what could appear to be obvious: after the decision to intervene and a period of preparation, all engagement of forces takes place across three phases. The first, called intervention, aims to "impose temporary order by using force to conquer violence and chaos". During this phase where we agree "win the battle", military actions dominate over diplomacy. As soon as the situation is the slightest bit controlled, a phase of stabilization is begun, which aims to "consolidate the transitory order previously imposed by reducing and then containing the violence, in order to allow for everyone to commit to the road to peace". If the military is still present to contribute to security, all of the other crisis management actors really get into the reconstruction project; this is the phase during which the comprehensive approach is supposed to develop. Finally, a last phase, normalization, aims to "put in place and strengthen a political, legal and social system that is sustainable and accepted by the protagonists of the conflict". Intervention-stabilization-normalization: this implacable logic seems particularly convincing when it takes the form of a blueprint: however, it empirically poses a serious problem when the enemy isn't wearing a uniform and when no defeat has been recognized by the opponent to determine the passage from one phase to the following. The evolution of violence makes this continuum outdated since the conditions to pass from the intervention phase to the stabilization phase are never assembled. Said differently, the initial intervention doesn't necessarily create the conditions that allow for the emergence of stabilization or normalization: it therefore becomes impossible to implement the comprehensive approach. Concretely, in order to establish a calmer political discourse, the intervening country highlights the comprehensive approach in order to show its desire to not limit itself to the military component;

however, this comprehensive approach needs a calm security environment to be able to spread. For lack of freedom of movement and in order to not complicate the situation by becoming hostages, the actors within the comprehensive approach remain prisoners in military camps or secured areas in the capitals. On the other side, keen to meet political ambitions but aware of the reality on the ground, members of the general staff take measures to accompany the steady progress of the passage from the intervention phase to the stabilization phase. In this way, the few humanitarians who are ready to "compromise" themselves through contact with the armed forces can be seen offering escorts and security arrangements that are in the end quite dangerous because they are very predictable. Out of desperation, militaries are trying to do themselves what should have been done by others. This is the time of CIMIC[4] operations and of the humanitarian solider, who provokes a lack of comprehension and disappointment on the parts of all the protagonists. We would like to be persuaded that the effects skillfully coordinated by military and development activities allow for the showing of a balanced and ambitious image of intervention. In fact, trying to develop a comprehensive approach while the situation has not stabilized tends to inhibit the actors and make intervention unclear.

---

4. *Civilian military cooperation* (CIMIC): aid given to a population as a way of encouraging them to accept armed forces.

We do not want to give the impression that that we favor a strictly military approach. Far from it: the combination of military and civil action is crucial to reach the desired level of stability. Nevertheless, it seems that the comprehensive approach has the objective of compensating for the absence of objectives and political strategies with an apparently generous morality. Although it is regularly raised in strategy, it does not today form a way of successfully understanding operations. At the interdepartmental level, as on the ground, one of the main limits of its implementation, a guarantee of the political rules of conflicts, lies in the incapability of coordinating all the actors needed for the settlement of conflicts: the necessarily single nature of effort and leadership is rarely the norm; the armed forces who are often responsible for its implementation have difficulty achieving this. This attempt of application inevitably involves a blurriness around the perimeters and a dissolution of the responsibilities that are detrimental to the general efficiency of the operation. The comprehensive approach imagines, mistakenly, that it can give a moral direction to military action; when it's brutally imposed outside of a favorable context, the comprehensive approach scrambles the message of military action and damages its efficiency. It places the military in an impossible and unreadable situation in the eyes of local populations. In the end, this concept appears more relevant upstream, in order to predict crises, than downstream, to settle them. Let us once again quote Lars Apfel: "Conceptually, this approach is linked to the inherent tendency that our societies have to take advantage of occasions to shape the world according to their own vision. But for this path to have success, it implies the rallying forward of everyone." This not being the case, it seems urgent to start afresh with this concept.

2.

The Myth of Counterterrorist Targeting

Faced with the inefficiency of interventions aiming to restore sovereignty to "failed states" and the central nature of the terrorist threat, the first approach now in fashion in the strategic community aims to make counterterrorism the primary objective of our interventions. This approach has the benefit of an apparent ease. It involves quite simply the fighting of terrorism in the places where it's found. Like a doctor faced with metastasis, it concerns the destruction of the terrorist cells alone, while minimizing the impact on the rest of the social body.

Militarily speaking, "surgical" actions are in this way favored. Made possible by precise and targeted information, these actions favor the use of strikes with metrical precision. If a presence on the ground is necessary to guide the strikes and evaluate them in assessments, the rule is to minimize their "imprint" by prioritizing the use of special forces. If, for reasons of efficiency, it's necessary to resort to local forces, the use of proxies[1] is of course considered, as this has massively been the case in the war against Daesh in Iraq, Syria and Libya.

Legally speaking, judicial structures allow for the joining of these actions into the framework of international law. Often, self-defense is claimed in order to justify the destruction of terrorist cells in countries against which we are not officially at war. It is never very difficult to show that a terrorist cell is in collaboration with a group which has been implicated in attacks on national territory. In any case, the general consensus is that we must fight Daesh or any other threat that is categorized as "terrorist", and rare are the people who dare object to anything that resembles a national cause.

The advantages of this anti-terrorist approach, more often called a "counter-terrorist approach" or a "CT approach", are many. Politically, it allows for the executive government to prove its resolve against terrorism, at a very low cost. At the other end of what the "Afghan quagmire" represented, where French soldiers were physically committed on the ground, targeted warfare allows for the unthinkable: dealing with a threat with precision, without putting oneself uselessly at risk and proving the results, with photos to back them up. The results, expressed in the number of destroyed enemies, are "objectificable", therefore, transferable. In the media, the CT approach is eye-catching. Beyond the captivating power exercised by videos of targeted

1. These might be local institutional partners or not.

strikes, communication is even more manageable since access to war zones are more and more difficult for journalists to gain entrance. This feeling of a clean war thus prevails, a war without useless atrocities. This vision of war, at the polar opposite of the frightening stories told by Ernst Jünger or the apocalyptic images from the Second World War, arouses little emotion in western public opinion, only too happy to be able to continue living a normal life. The last advantage is the extremely light French losses. Nonetheless, the death of a special forces fighter always seems more "acceptable" in the eyes of public opinion. It passes as a non-event in the chain of continuous news stories, the obvious reasons of the security of the operations often preventing the release of the smallest detail. In short, "CT" warfare seems to have become, for some, the alpha and the omega of military intervention today. It seems like the perfect match of military response with political ambition, more or less directly reflected in the expectations of the voting base.

That being said, the reader might have already understood that we do not share this enthusiasm for this strategy, which tends, nonetheless, to be seen as the new paradigm.

First of all, the counterterrorist approach does not attack the roots of the evil: it only occasionally deals with a symptom. The origins of the crises with which we are familiar lies notably in the propagation of radical ideologies, the decay of states, former antagonisms or the failure of the tools of supranational governments.

However, it is certain that the counterterrorist approach only attacks the surface of things: the metastases, not the cancer itself. In effect, nothing proves that the heads of terrorist groups systematically constitute the heart of the enemy. The first difficulty of this method lies, additionally, in the formation of the list of targets to be destroyed: is it better to aim at the tactical leaders, the leaders at the intermediary level, the ideologies that preach for revolt, the recruiters, those who finance these groups...? Doubts on this subject reveal the confusion facing the definition of the nature of the enemy and facing the complexity of the local situation. Some will object that in the absence of miracle solutions, this approach is a last resort, a way of containing the threat, in lieu of handling it. In fact, along with the tracking of terrorists, there is nothing that prevents the pursuit of diplomatic negotiations to find a political solution to the crisis. This is the de facto choice that prevails today over scenes of crises, notably in Syria. However, history teaches us that, deprived of its main lever, which is war, diplomacy will always have trouble bringing together enemy agendas.

The second reason to feel a certain skepticism about the counterterrorist approach is with its reliance on the misconception that a surgical war at a low cost exists, it tends to make commonplace the use of force: the distinction between a state of war and a state of non-war gradually disappears. Beyond legitimate ethical considerations, this means considering a resort to armed action as a non-event. It becomes therefore politically rational to use it for its indirect effects on domestic policy, rather than to limit its use while searching for a political solution in times of crises. The normalization of war, despite everything, tends to emphasize what should be considered a limited approach.

The third reason and not the least of them, is that the image that we send of the western world constantly resorting to this new way of making war is often disastrous, especially after the first phase of intervention, during which it seems legitimate to "pull out all the stops". There is, of course, the cowardly trial made against drone pilots, those men who "give death without accepting the idea of putting their own lives in danger", breaking, in fact, the moral contract of reciprocity which united, in the past, all the soldiers of the world. This trial has little importance, in and of itself; it appears each time that a new weapon can little by little, drive enemies away from each other. But the apparently "clean" aspect of leading the war underestimates, in reality, the immense violence of this process: along with the possibility of being struck without prior warning and the elimination of a battle front or confrontation, local populations experience feelings of intrusion, violation and even cowardice that will ultimately harm the achieving of the final objectives. The Israeli researcher Martin van Creveld, in The Transformation of War, perfectly explains the limits of this remote war. According to him, the outcome of battle is only recognized and accepted—therefore, does not make up a prerequisite for reconciliation and reconstruction—if the two armies are mostly equivalent or in any case, if the two armies have the possibility of winning. If not, the conquered will not recognize its defeat because it will consider that the enemy camp has not demonstrated its commitment nor its courage. On the other side, the conqueror has the feeling of being morally unable to claim its victory and thus to demand the benefits, if it hasn't literally faced the enemy. Would Goliath have admitted his pride if he'd killed David? Would we still be talking about it today? We find here the paradoxical notion that to be really "winnable", a conflict must be equally "losable"! Thus, resorting to technology and maneuvers that distance the western fighter from his enemy has a long-term counterproductive effect, even if its uses can be perfectly understood from a military, political or media point of view. More serious is the idea, now well anchored, that the western world never respects the rules that it imposes, by force, on the rest of the world. Populations that were initially very separate from terrorists often come to "understand" their reasons, while the inevitable collateral damages and disrespect of state sovereignty quickly make them forget the legitimate motives that had motivated western intervention. The antiterrorist war feeds a very real resentment and increases identity tensions in people who were already very aware that their civilization had not managed to create a "model" that could directly compete with the western model.

Finally, we must recognize that after fifteen years of "CT war", it seems that our frenzy to cut off heads has had only two real consequences: it has made jihadist social mobility work and it has given terrorist groups the opportunity to unite against a common enemy. In fact, with the possible exceptions of the neutralizing of emblematic leaders like Iyad Ag Ghaly or Mokhtar Belmokhtar, the targeting of these infamous "HVTs" (high-value targets) doesn't lead to the end of terrorist groups; it only modifies the terrorist ecosystem by making new heads appear. It also helps the terrorist recruitment pool grow, notably among families of assassinated terrorists, by providing a convenient image of a common enemy: the West.

For all of these reasons, the virtues of what we have called the "CT" approach must be qualified. This doesn't mean that this approach is completely senseless. It is the modern avatar of what Israelis call "a lawnmower blow": in the absence of an immediate political solution between Israel and Palestine, the Israel Defense Forces know that they must come down to the Gaza Strip on a regular basis and cut off "the bad heads" in order to artificially maintain a delicate peace. Our "CT war" has some points in common with this approach. Very often, it switches the pre-eminence bestowed upon the short-term to the long-term. It can, without a doubt, occasionally contribute to the objectives of force but its action should not be over-evaluated so that it becomes a fully-fledged strategy. Finally, let's remember that from a political point of view, the idea that a "CT option" allows us to politically benefit through minimal use of the military is generally speaking, an illusion. Overall, the political dividends are proportional to the military effort.

3.

The Coalition Conundrum

An idea that emerges in public debate is the necessity of forming coalitions. In fact, it is today commonly accepted that the national level is now overwhelmed; experts agree that for political, military and financial reasons, future operations will systematically be led in coalitions, either "made to measure" (ad hoc coalitions) or institutional (within the framework of the UN, the EU or NATO).

On first look, there's nothing about this that's especially groundbreaking. What could be more normal than to look for allies to share the financial, human, moral and psychological efforts of a war? A coalition provides more of a chance for success through the extra numbers it brings; it also reassures, making us feel that the cause being defended must be fair and noble if other allies are willing to contribute. Additionally, the historical perspectives seems to show that since the Trojan War, the majority of large interventions throughout history have seen confrontations between coalitions, whether we're talking about the Napoleonic Wars, the World

Wars or, more recently, the engagements in Afghanistan, Iraq or Syria.

This systematic orientation towards coalition engagements seems also to be linked with the logic of European armies having available armies whose numbers are few and whose materials, while certainly of high quality, are used in "sample sizes". Seeing the budgets that European countries devote to their defense, the idea of pooling and sharing costs naturally seems attractive; it would allow for financial and human savings but also savings in terms of the efforts and the wear and tear of armies. This step seems all the more fair if, as we think of it, current engagements have a tendency to occur over a long period of time.

The idea of a coalition also assumes a psychological interest. Western public opinion being hesitant when it comes to military operations, those in political power like to be able to take shelter behind the force of the group, which is less suspected of hiding the shameful goals of war. International legitimacy is reassuring: participating in a coalition allows for the reinforcement of the image of the international responsibility of a state, especially when it relies on a UN resolution.

Finally, for European states, coalitions seem today to perfectly line up with defense strategies. If France expresses a desire to lead operations alone and maintain its ability to "enter first", it also insists on the controlling role of the Atlantic Alliance and on its ambition to see emerge a Europe of defense or a communal defense of Europe. This ambition is especially significant today.

It seems clear enough that the United States, without losing interest in Africa, is not concentrating its efforts on this continent and is leaving to Europeans, and notably to France, the job of taking in hand the question of its security. When it comes to immigration, threats of attack and drug and weapons trafficking, it seems obvious that the tensions which cross through the Maghreb and the Sahel have negative repercussions on all European countries, not just France or Italy. What then would be more logical than for European countries to support France in its military efforts against terrorist threats within the framework of Operation Barkhane? Today however, aid from France's neighboring countries is limited to logistical support from Germany and from others, the sending of small contingents in non-combat areas: medical support, training...

In any case, resorting to coalitions cannot become a slogan which hides the respective shortcomings of the states: adding up weaknesses does not create strength! The efficiency of a multinational operation does not happen by decree and responds to specifications made complicated by the national particularities of the intervening countries and especially by the perspective of the host country: this argument is often forgotten. The goal is not, for all that, to rant against coalitions by making them the champions of all things national. Quite the opposite.

One of the first mistakes is believing that coalitions are created around consensus on the goals of a war and that this initial agreement will allow for further agreement on how to design the operation, the intermediary objectives and the question of leadership. A coalition is created around a nation and it's this nation that sets the tone of an operation. France is happy to think up coalitions...on the condition that it can impose its views and therefore that it will have real control, even if it hides this desire behind a smokescreen of collegiality. This patriotic reflex is doubtless evidence of efficiency. In conflicts where the survival of the states is not at stake, the functioning of coalitions clashes with the restrictions, distinctive identities and prides of each of the participating states. These restrictions, called "caveats", are the area in which each state will preserve its political freedom of action, less to erase rough patches while preparing for common success than to confirm its sovereignty. In this way, each country will adopt its own conditions for opening fire, will develop its own aerial terms and conditions or its vision of what should be the future local army and how to train it.

Without delving into these considerations, which reveal the profound nature of a state and the meaning that it wishes to give to its intervention, interventions by coalitions are particularly difficult to make concrete. The ability of military units to work together efficiently is based on numerous criteria which go beyond the mere inter-operability of communications, which is nonetheless seen as the ultimate stage. To be effective, units must have at their disposal the same procedures, shared training and ideally, a mutual understanding that goes far beyond the simple exchange of liaison offers between general staffs. Today, France directly works with Americans the most: the NATO framework has provided a shared melting pot; the status of framework nation of the United States in Afghanistan is evident and has pushed France to align itself with their procedures. In Europe, France has maintained a privileged relationship with Great Britain, ever since the Lancaster House Treaties and completes regular shared trainings that make credible a possible later engagement in a coalition. With other European countries, France carries out exchanges that are more or less deepened but it would be an exaggeration to say that these states are ready to commit to a shared intervention.

To this end, the voluntaristic European discourse that dreams of a European army in the short term, seeing here a "small step", an additional "de facto cooperation", is debatable. There is no area more sovereign than that of defense and no state is ready to back off in this area without a threat forcing them to do so. A shared army will be able to put the finishing touches on a political creation but will not be able to create the conditions. Today, European armies' visions are too different to imagine that they could share goals of war. France is one of the only countries, along with Great Britain, to maintain a culture of expeditionary forces. Eastern and northern European countries remain oriented towards the Heartland[1]. Nowadays, the question of terrorism is

1. The Heartland Theory is the name of a geopolitical analysis offered by English geographer Halford John Mackinder at the start of the 20th century. The Heartland is a geographical area located

not perceived with the same degree of urgency in Rome, Oslo or Vienna, even if the question of immigration is giving a new topicality to the subject. These differences in perception also have consequences on the materials used or the doctrines followed. It's difficult to imagine Eastern European countries massively committing themselves in the Sahel; it is, certainly, possible to imagine that they will contribute to an operation in order to show support or a desire to have more influence; on the other hand, it seems hardly credible that they could greatly influence something like this.

This thought leads to reflection on the legitimacy of action, not in legal terms but in terms of acceptance by the host country's population. The African countries with which France has a shared history ultimately have a simple enough relationship with the former colonial power. They can denigrate its role and attribute current evils to colonization or the brutality of their independences; they can also regret certain aspects of this era and consider it normal for France to act as "the police officer of Africa". But in all cases, they agree on recognizing "a common destiny". Old links exist; they create a proximity, a privileged relationship, which justifies a marked interest and trust. In Africa, France is counted on and generally welcomed. But this particular connection is split with difficulty. The case of northern Mali is

---

between the Volga and the Yangtze. According to Mackinder, "who rules East Europe commands the Heartland; who rules the Heartland commands the World-Island; who rules the World-Island commands the world."

particularly interesting. The Tuareg people disapprove of France's choice, as interpreted through Operation Barkhane; they consider this unjustified support for Bamako, meaning for the tribes in southern Mali. For all that, the Tuareg people know enough about their history to not find it abnormal that France would be interested in this part of the world; they're also convinced that France will inevitably be an interested party in the solution that will emerge. This is true for phases of intervention but, even more, for the very sensitive post-crisis phase, where an ancient understanding and a reciprocal trust are not too much to hope for in order to come to a viable situation.

In view of this analysis, it seems illusory to think that European countries have an equal responsibility and that, reciprocally, they will be received in the same way by host countries. What is valid for the Danish and the Polish in Niger is still truer for the Bangladeshi or Cambodgians engaged in Mali within the framework of UNmissions! The legitimacy of the intervener is determined in the initial phase of chaos and threat which decides the intervention. It is still more decisive in the phase of reconstruction that follows: it's one thing to see foreign armed forces on their soil; it's another to accept and receive, on their part, advice in all of the areas that determine the life of a state. Missions dubbed "hit and transfer" or "bridging operations" must be appreciated without subterfuge. We must label as a myth the belief that a unit which isn't implicated in an initial coercive phase has the right to lead pursuit of the mission, all while allowing the "first responder" nation to leave the territory. From a strictly national point of view, these bridging operations can perfectly be justified, notably to accelerate a departure if a stalemate is inevitable. And yet, the fact remains that the probability of armed forces, be they local, regional or foreign, be able to successfully take the on-site reins is extremely small. This is, for example, the case of Operation Sangaris in the Central African Republic; designed to be a bridging operation, this option allowed France to repatriate its armed forces in good conditions. The current instability seems, despite everything, to demonstrate that UN forces have trouble, despite their efforts, to efficiently take the reins.

In conclusion, if it's likely that future interventions will take place for the most part in coalitions, these coalitions are not a panacea. In particular, we must not confuse a coalition with a kind of badly understood multinational collegiality. In the interests of efficiency as with the respect of legitimate local susceptibilities, the place of different intervening nations and the nature of their contributions should be approached with pragmatism, taking into account the weight of history, as well as the nature and force of the connections that unite the host country with the intervening country. This is crucial for the nation that takes on command but this also applies to contributing nations. Partners should not necessarily be looked for among our historical allies; these partners must, above all, be sought among the countries (or possibly the infra-state armed groups) that demonstrate real motivation. This motivation, far from the media buzz and the lone question of means, may be easily understood by posing the following question: "Is my ally ready to sacrifice soldiers' lives for the intervention that I wish to lead?" The answer to this simple question allows for no mistakes. From a political point of view, let us remember that the more limited the political stakes, as is the norm today, the more fragile coalitions are.

4.

The Dilemma of Local Situations

One of the more widely accepted opinions today is that local solutions should be favored. This idea has almost become a slogan by dint of repetition. It might seem paradoxical in this paper to criticize the notion after previous chapters, where we denigrated interventions disconnected from terrain realities and observed the long-term inefficiency of western interventions. It is a seemingly difficult idea to contest, insofar as it is based on reasons that are as much philosophical as empirical, and which seem to bring the best guarantees of justice and long-term success. And yet, the road to hell is paved with good intentions, and it does not seem unjustified to look more precisely at this idea to show that it too can have counterproductive results.

This statement is first of all based on reasons of image. Repeated on the international level all the way down to the lowest tactical levels, it firstly provides a defense against the widely disseminated and very destructive image of western countries being overly confident and convinced of the soundness of their own solutions. Western countries, and primarily France, see the occasion to exorcise the specter of crippling accusations of neocolonialism. This position also reflects the desire of western states to present themselves as promoters of international legality and even-handed dignity of peoples and nations. This is especially true for France which, all while maintaining a marked interest in countries of former French West Africa (Afrique occidentale française) and French Equatorial Africa (Afrique équatoriale française), wants to also show that the era of Françafrique is over.

Beyond its rhetorical and reassuring aspect, asserting the preeminence of local solutions is linked with a difficult-to-contest empirical statement, namely that the complexity of local situations demand the participation of local actors, who have an acute understanding of local power struggles that would escape the western mind, especially when carrying out short mandates in a given territory. This deepened understanding of the social fabric remains especially complicated despite efforts to explain, to simplify and to categorize on the part of a few researchers or the aid of travel journals written by camel officers in the previous century! Despite their willingness to learn, western countries often create harmful confusions: taking ethnic loyalty as nepotism, commerce for trafficking, a feudal line for subjected humiliation, considering a meeting to be a decision-making place... Generally speaking, western countries have trouble leaving behind a “meritocratic” logic, which is rarely the only one that prevails in the countries of intervention.

Additionally, the solutions suggested by local actors might be more easily accepted by the population than would those from a foreign army which would not be able to protect itself from accusations of manipulation, severity or more simply, misunderstanding.
Additionally, the failure of solutions totally or partially "off the ground" is not under debate, which also seems to favor local solutions. Many examples of this approach can be evoked. The most caricatured one is that of the purely exogenous solution: faced with a threat, a western state intervenes without really taking into account the reality of the situation or local issues, and without trying to encourage the local political situation; this typically calls to mind the 2011 military intervention in Libya. The second example is pushing for a solution that to all appearance is the "local solution", but in reality possesses few aspects of that. This calls to mind the cases of Afghanistan and Iraq: President Karzai, like Prime Minister Al-Maliki, are very much local political personalities but they have been insisted upon, more or less delicately, by the "occupier"; having no legitimacy initially, be it from the people, tribes or warriors, President Karzai and Prime Minister Al-Maliki will never be able to rid themselves of the unflattering appearance of being American "puppets". On the contrary, it seems that the willingness to place local actors on the front lines increases the likelihood that sustainable solutions will be found. This option has the merit of not deluding ourselves as regards the accepting of the foreign force and its imposed solutions, as good as they might be.

This leitmotif of "local solutions" seems solidly grounded. It has often been theorized under the term "inclusive solutions". Nevertheless, it clashes with the difficulty of implementation, often due to an excess of idealism!

The initial mistake consists of underestimating the inherent violence of a "failed" country undergoing a crisis, no matter what kind. In the chaos linked to the absence of institutions, and the weak perspective that they bring to light in the short term, the local actors that emerge are, in general, the most determined and in that time, the most violent; this violence of the actors and the radical nature of the local solutions proposed creates unease for the western country. After a phase of intervention that is relatively violent, the western country would like there to emerge a less tense climate, with leaders chosen by consensus and peaceful solutions; this seems more in line with its campaign and the image that it would like to send back to the international community as well as to its own public. However, the intervention, if it is permitted to momentarily calm tensions, has in no way settled the tribal, political and economic problems at their core. The panel of local actors, the "strong men" on which western countries could rely, often bears little resemblance to the profile initially conceived by the chancelleries. There is an elevated risk, in the name of respectable moral values, of having to refuse local solutions that are judged unacceptable, undemocratic or not respecting human rights. Ideology retakes the upper hand and leads one to forget the axiom previously accepted: western intervention should be accompanied by the emerging of a local actor, but the intervention should not choose an actor who doesn't have a strong local base and popular support. It's quite common to see denials of any cultural influence in the waging of war and of the leading role played by violence within conflict settlement in "failed States". In short, flattering ourselves that we have supported local solutions becomes difficult when the solutions chosen are shocking to western values!

Another mistake is a lack of clear-headedness when it comes to the capacity of local actors to create realistic solutions and then implement them. Faced with the necessity of finding "local solutions", all while taking into account the state of decay and disorganization in "local security forces", it's common to think of resolving the equation through training. We do not want to show contempt for this idea, which can indeed be one of the conditions for improvement. However, it's important to remain lucid about what we can expect from an investment in this area. An army can rebuild itself in a few years provided that it possesses a military culture, significant means, well-established frameworks and especially, a strong political willingness. These conditions are very rarely fulfilled in the countries where France intervenes. These training sessions aim to fulfill objectives like building an army that is capable of "taking up the torch" and "taking on the responsibility for security". It is an illusion to think that this training will allow for the army of a "failed State", prey as it is to internal divisions, to attain a level superior to its previous situation. The training aims therefore to legitimize the power in place by giving it the illusion of having sovereign rights, limiting the degradation of the local army and channeling a part of the violence into a pseudo-institutional framework. Naturally, the training aims also to maintain reserve forces that are capable of executing missions of limited scope, either alone or accompanied by western detachments. Generally speaking, the idea of local troops being accompanied by western forces is one of the major reasons the former is willing to invest in these trainings. The absence of perspective in this area transforms trainings into fragile and barely profitable veneers. This is even truer when the training is carried out by western contingents from multiple nationalities who quickly come one after the other in the same setting, without any real follow-up. Finally, the "search for a local solution" sometimes summarizes itself in an elegant formula that tries to hide a pressing desire for withdrawal. However, the local actors, like the local populations, have enough clarity to understand that a local solution will only have the chance of succeeding if it is supported by western forces. Local actors consider, quite rightly, that since the state has decided to intervene, it must also ensure a kind of "after-sales service"; they are not anticipating an abrupt withdrawal of the country that led the intervention, even if political leaders will sometimes adopt this discourse in order to flatter the African-ness of their electorate. On the contrary, the emergence of a "doable" local solution requires an abundance of energy to assemble different local actors and have them work, even if they're opposed to each other: but, in the disorganized states, only the country that led the intervention is generally capable of playing this role. This is also why the "local solution" which consists of appealing to a regional organization, like the African Union for example, is not a panacea. This solution is inevitable but it might not be enough. Basically, this organization could play an important role in mediation that no European country could take on but at the same time, it would make no sense to imagine that this organization would have the legitimacy, willingness and capacity to ensure the replacement of a western country in security terms as well as aid and development terms.

Therefore, it seems that this slogan extolling "local solutions" possesses a part of the truth, in the sense that certain aspects of understanding and crisis resolution will always escape the intervening country. But this slogan should not lead us to think that interventions are not necessary and that host countries have the internal resources and motivations necessary to settle contentious situations. The strength of western armies should consist of helping produce these local solutions and then accompanying them.

*

At the end of this analysis, we have tried to show that the assessment of external interventions should be questioned. A lot of militaries are not necessarily at ease with this step; this is understandable. After all, political power asks of armies to lead limited conflict, with constrained ambitions and means. They do it with a remarkable cost-effectiveness, often much better than that of our American ally. Once again, the goal is not to judge here the efficiency of militaries as actors on the ground, an area in which a trial on inefficiency would be especially ill-timed. The political authorities who succeed each other at the head of the Ministry of the Armed Forces or who visit units in France as if they're on a mission do not generally make errors about this. The objective is to determine if the conditions in which armies intervene allow for, ultimately, the attaining of the desired strategic and political objectives.

When all is said and done, isn't the main pitfall wanting to think in the system too much or simply wanting to describe the process which, by its nature, is bound to be chaotic? Doesn't true efficiency lie in the capacity to understand the real rather than to dream it? To this end, is a new approach necessary? It's not the lack of political ambition nor the lack of means which make the comprehensive approach unworkable today. If tomorrow, billions of Euros were poured into the accounts of the Sahel and the numbers of soldiers were multiplied by ten, it is not absolutely certain that Malian political problem would be settled. This means that we have a problem of strategic efficiency. Our soldiers can certainly be efficient locally, on the ground, but can't our modes of action, as such, be optimized? Will our soldiers be ready when one day, they face better equipped and better trained opponents? Are our structures of command and our way of dealing with conflict adapted and adaptable? Are we capable of surpassing the identified limits of the comprehensive approach? And finally, is it undeniable that bureaucratization touches all the institutions of the world, is it a pretext to be satisfied with it within general staffs, who give the impression of being as big as the units that they direct?

We have tried up until now to demonstrate that, faced with repeated failures and the resurgence of threats on our national territory, certain ideologies, notably neoconservative myths, have been abandoned. Unfortunately, the paradigms of substitution which have quickly seen the light of day have shown their limitations, leaving western societies unarmed for thinking about their interventions effectively. The collective tendency to replace myths with other myths lies, above all, in the difficulty of responding to the complexity of situations being encountered today. Since everything is going quickly, since everyone is aware of it, since the power to say yes or no is shared between many actors, the states seem to be prisoners of the process that they themselves invented, going so far as to be condemned to remain in perpetual reaction when faced with events, without being able to anticipate, nor influence them.

In light of all this, we are convinced that "the worst error is to not see the world as it is". Offering roads of reflections to increase the efficiency of interventions should, above all, start with an analysis of how to understand that complexity.

Looking for a New Approach

What can we propose that hasn't already been offered? The first chapters sought to show that the efficiency of interventions could be optimized, then we looked more deeply into the causes, particularly analyzing the role of the comprehensive approach which seems simultaneously the cause and the indicator of the inefficiency of current interventions. This analysis echoes numerous other writings produced by observers of international relations, which have already been alluded to previously. The risk is therefore great, that in this, our attempt, we might fall into different traps: that of ease, cautiously settling for the pronouncement of a few large general principles; that of trend, proposing a better interdepartmental or interagency coordination via the creation of a new cell or a more systematic recourse to special forces; that of demagogy, in asking for more means for the armies.

It is to avoid this bias that a last reflection on the complexity seems necessary. In fact, the common denominator amongst all of these reflections when approaching the question of efficiency in external operation seems to lie in this idea that the situations we encounter and the processes that we follow to change the direction of the course taken by these interventions has become, at this point, so complex that we have the impression that we're being sentenced to a choice between inhibition and brutality.

I.

Getting Used to Complexity

For almost a century, when globalization was still a long way away, enlightened observers of the world have been highlighting the world's growing complexity. Paul Valéry put it this way: "Instead of playing with destiny as at one time, we would have played an honest game of cards, knowing the number of cards and characters, we now find ourselves in the situation of a player who realizes with astonishment that his partner's hand gives him never before seen characters and that the rules of the game have changed with each turn. There is no probability theory that is possible here and he can't even throw his cards at the nose of his partner."[1] The complexity that we know is, when compared to previous generations, exacerbated by immediacy, real time and media coverage. Faced with this complexity which, for example, makes it so that a broadcast photo of a dead child on the beach can provoke profound emotions in European countries and influence immigration politics,

1. Paul Valéry, *Regards sur le monde actuel*, Rev. ed. (Gallimard, 1961)

the positioning of decision-makers tends to be polarized. On one side, those who are the most assured of the validity of their cause tend to sacrifice a part of this complexity, to the detriment of a basic kind of prudence. On the other side, the most cautious adopt the opposite position: for fear of not mastering the consequences of an action, they prefer solutions involving compromise, even large displays, at the risk of not being able to reach their objectives. In the end, two extremes take shape: acting with brutality to "twist reality" or resigning oneself to "doing one's best". This dualism does not allow for the emerging of a new way of thinking of our relationship with interventions. In fact, it pushes us to think that when faced with encountered situations and the national ambitions that arise from them, everything is a question of political commitment: "If we really want to reach an objective, we'll provide the means for it!" we might think. This need for balance between political ambition and agreed-upon means is real, but it seems exaggerated to consider it as the only criterion. We cannot make the success of an intervention rely solely on the political implication; this criterion isn't enough to explain the lack of efficiency. When considering this need to create coherence among political objectives, military objectives and the means being used, we must add a method, an approach. Before thinking about this, let us leave behind anything that might compel as to approach this complexity as nothing other than an obstacle. We must reconnect it with efficiency and not consider it only as a "non-conforming case", an error emerging from the execution of the plan; rather, we must understand it be an unavoidable reality that we must accept, in order to make better use of it. Could we even go so far as to make this managed complexity an asset?

Removing the False Choice Between Inhibition and Brutality

This question of complexity firstly poses a challenge to the relevance of intervention. In a highly evocative way, intervening in a foreign country seems like a game of playing God, during which, after having struck with its initial action, the intervening state examines the consequences of these actions, before then wearing itself out in trying to contain the resulting unwanted effects. There emerges a feeling of radical uncertainty when faced with the possible evolution of actions that we undertake in the host systems of our interventions. We will naturally be able to object that at the moment of passing from thought into action, we must decide for a certain simplification in order to identify a doable option and to not remain inhibited in the face of uncertainty. This Gordian Knot theory, which would be necessary to slice through is acceptable but it means admitting to decide to be the "bull in a china shop", while assuring ourselves that the quantity of destroyed china remains coherent with the level of political implication... However, the recent examples of interventions which wished to flout the reality of local complexities in order to impose, by force, off-soil solutions, does not seem to favor this theory. The opposite option, pushed to its extreme, would consist of ceaselessly weighing the options, evaluating the probabilities, imagining contingencies, all to finally refuse to engage oneself, for lack of guarantees. Instead of resigning oneself to this alternative, it might be interesting, on the contrary, to take note of this complexity and try to rethink the place of armed action in it. This does not mean proving that there is no longer a place for war. It remains the main mode of settling conflicts on a large part of the planet. It also doesn't mean making armed intervention a banal event. Rather, it means identifying the moments where interventions might be necessary and then identifying the ways in which to make them more useful and effective. At the minimum, it means studying the best way in which to avoid the stalemate that can define itself as the phase of an intervention during which an army is entrapped by the complexity of the ecosystem in which it is intervening.

Removing the Ideologically Correct

Faced with the complexity of a local situation, there might be a great temptation for a western mind, blinded by the feeling of its superiority, to look to transpose or impose the model that it knows. We often believe that if regional identities could find the means to express themselves through peaceful democracy, they would no longer act as sources of tension. The intervention cannot, however, have as an objective the creation of a better world; it cannot, in a few years, manage a political restructuring. It seems absolutely urgent to stray from the "ideologically correct"[2], which seems like a denial of complexity. The "ideologically correct" does not allow us to rely on the stabilization mechanisms that are grounded in other things besides the usual institutions: ethnic groups, ancient allegiances. An approach that is grounded in the most deeply anchored cultural and social reality, in "the profound forces", seems therefore necessary. For, if we push aside the brutal and not very effective idea of changing regimes[3], what can we lucidly expect from an intervention? Interventions will always consist of a modification in the power balances in favor of the intervening country, or, more often, of a partner or an ally; this change of power balances will allow for the strengthening or restoring of a local authority, of silencing a threat to find the status quo ante (the way things were before) or to force one of the present parties to return to the negotiation table: to attach other ambitions to an intervention seems illusory. As Aron reminds us: "It's never a conflict between good and evil, but always a choice between the preferable

2. Expression used by Philippe Gros in an interview with *Paroles d'Actu*, entitled: Volet militaire de la guerre contre l'EI : quelle cohérence stratégique ? (Parolesdactu.canalblog.com).

3. The American term often used is "regime change".

and the detestable."[4] However, in this framework, it's often difficult to express what is "preferable", especially when it involves supporting a dictator. It is therefore important to not expect from an intervention more than it is capable of producing: the intervention must take all of its space, but nothing more than its space. Does this analysis discredit the principle of interventions? Do interventions represent too great of a risk? Do they constitute an anachronism? We do not believe so. If the complexity can be assessed in terms of risk, it can also be translated into terms of opportunity. However, this means adapting our blueprints, adjusting them in order to incorporate the idea that complexity is the norm and not a collapse of planning. Faced with the inability to determine the medium and long term consequences of an intervention, committing to a goal of war and then going backwards from there to deduce the main deadlines and actions to lead, seems like an impossible mission or like pride. We must have the humility to admit that we can't expect host countries' political restructurings from interventions: that can only happen after a long process of political maturation. The success of an intervention that was destined to stabilize a country can only be assessed within a reasonable time of a few years; a period of time that varies, of course, depending on the intervention.

4. Raymond Aron, *Le spectateur engagé* (Julliard, 1981)

Abandoning the Idea that Bureaucracy Can be Escaped

We have already discussed the risk of bureaucracy. It would therefore be a little dishonest, in a chapter dedicated to complexity to limit ourselves to describing the complexity of situations or approaches, while forgetting to bring up the internal complexity of our own organizations and systems. Western organizations are greatly complicated and it's difficult to complete reforms on them that would allow for the simplification of decision-making processes. Bureaucracy has multiple causes. For this essay, let's stick with the idea that complexity can lead the way to a specialization that results in working in silos; there will be an attempt to correct with a coordination center that will try to reestablish coherence and dialogue; but this center will develop its own working processes, which will then become an additional workload. Past a certain stage, situations stop being thought about in terms of reality, instead being looked at in terms of administrative processes. The democratic system is, by definition, sensitive to this bureaucratic tendency; the different powers, the highest civil servants, the departmental and administrative directors make up just as many opposing powers which are developing an autonomy that doesn't favor working together. These differences in perception, this "vanity fair", to take an expression of General de Gaulle, in the operation of large administrations, can lead to a complication that feeds bureaucracy. Finally, as Max Weber points out, we might consider that the welfare state, through the expanding of the state's prerogatives in all social domains, directly contributes to bureaucratization. Our objective here is not to rise up against this state of affairs because bureaucracy seems like the inevitable corollary to large communities. If it is commendable and necessary to fight this tendency, it seems on the other hand naïve to consider that we can achieve, in the medium-term, remarkable progress in this area. The issue thus consists less in resolving this problem than in bypassing it: looking for a situational "alignment of the planets" rather than a structural reform. Stated differently, the efficiency of interventions will require the putting into place of an exceptional situation where decision-making will not follow the usual movements.

Getting out of the Politico-Military Conflict

Our reflection on complexity cannot skip over an important subject: that of the different perceptions we have of militaries and politicians; a perception that leads to caricatured visions of one and the other, as well as to harmful misunderstandings regarding the success of interventions. The meeting of these two rationalities, political and military, is humorously described by General Dempsey, former American Chief Staff of the Army, during a conference given at the Center for a New American Society in 2012: "The folks with whom we interact – that is to say, our elected officials – generally are more interested in what options they have when confronted with a problem. So the conversation goes something like this. — OK, General, we've got this problem, and we'd like you at the next meeting to present some options on how to address it. And then the general says: — OK, we can do that. What exactly are you trying to accomplish? What's the objective? And they say: — Well, before we know the objective, you know, we want to know how to take the first step. So what we'd really like you to do is come next time and help us understand the first step and maybe some limiting principles and how many options and at what varying degrees of risk. And then we say: — OK, we can do that, but where do you really want to end up? And I'm telling you, this can go on for months, actually. *(Laughter)* Right? And it doesn't mean that we're smart and they're not or they're smart and we're not. It's just we come at this literally from two very different cultures. [...] One of the things that I have learned is to find ways to bridge that gap between these two very different cultures and to also help educate our younger officers, the next generation of generals and admirals, because it can be a source of enormous frustration when we speak past each other about whether we start with options or we start with objectives."

This opposition between objectives on one side and options on the other reveals a state of mind that moves within, respectively, military and political environments: a fondness for "blurriness" that tends to disagree with the military rationale that is concerned with having clear objectives in order to construct its reasoning. The error, therefore, would be for the military to refuse to adapt itself to political logic, which favors prudence and transferability as it recalls alternative choice and exit routes. More serious and unlikely still would be to imagine the political world adapting itself to military software!

2.

Between Adapting to the Real and Long-Term Vision

Accepting Uncertainty

We have identified many of the reasons that prevent effectively adapting to complexity. How can we then approach this? Maybe by going to the very end of this logic; by accepting that complexity leads irreversibly to uncertainty. An interesting conceptual approach is offered by French philosopher Edgar Morin, who, in his work, elaborates on the foundations of "complex thought". He teaches that "no sooner are we initiated into a given environment, all action enters into a game of intersecting-retro-actions, which modify, divert and even invert the course. This eludes the will of its author."[1] Applied to our subject, this means that a country which intervenes today arrives in an extremely complicated system in which sub-sections (families, tribes) and issues (security, economic, societal) are inextricably combined.

1. Edgar Morin, *Introduction à la pensée complexe* (Le Seuil, 2005)

The actions that the intervening country goes to lead there will not only provoke direct effects on the sub-sections but these sub-sections will also interact amongst themselves in a way that is changing and unpredictable. All of these "intersecting-retro-actions" make the result of the intervention especially difficult to predict beyond the first sequences. This is even truer when the current way of dealing with complex problems relies on a mechanism of "disjunction" of the studied realities: in this way, the instability of a country is analyzed by economists from an economic angle, by the military from a security angle, by NGOs from a humanitarian angle... This studying in sections, this "slicing" of the object to be studied does not favor a correct understanding of phenomena in their complexities and encourages action in an ineffective way (in silos). Since it's difficult to look for a way of precisely measuring the consequences of our interventions, beyond the first sequences, how can we still arrange everything in function of the goal of war or an end state (état final recherché or EFR), the contemporary avatar? This forecasted step reaches its climax with the strategy called "effects-based operations" (EBO). This strategy, born during Operation Desert Storm in 1991, is today very common. The objective then was to develop a concept that was more adapted to conflicts in which there were significant differences in strength between the protagonists: a vision that was less Clausewitzien in which the destruction of opposing military capacities was no longer the ultimate objective. It also meant increasing the value of the role of the US

Air Force. This strategy, while intellectually relevant, led little by little to an excess of planning: the effect produced by a military action can be imagined but it nevertheless constitutes a fragile and difficult to predict base. Will the bombing of a unit lead to its neutralizing, reorienting or radicalizing? Will the targeting of a leader lead to the disorganization of a terrorist group or the emergence of a more effective successor? The analysis of the differentials between the expected effects and the real effects is the responsibility of the general staff but it's certain that this strategy severely tests their ability to adapt.[2] If Edgar Moran was speaking truth and unless we believe in the coming of supercalculators that will be able to sufficiently increase the cognitive capacities of overwhelmed human brains, it seems that we must not base excessive hopes in the definition of anend state. This doesn't mean that thinking about the goal of a war or its end state is useless. It does, however, mean that faced with our inability to predict what our actions will concretely produce and faced with the understandable and structural desire of our political authorities to not come down on one side or the other, we mustn't make the end state the sole determining factor of our plans and our means. Put differently, the fundamental question that we should agree needs to be resolved is: a strategy that doesn't ignore the end results but doesn't

2. This effects-based operations strategy is today being called into question in the United States.

use them as the only determining factor in its planning still see the light of day?

Should We Abandon a Strategy that is Entirely Based on the end state?

Let us first remember that this reflection might seem to contradict the military's need to plan and even the political preoccupation with clarity. The objective is not to denigrate the work of planning in favor of a logic of adaptation and management; its ambition is not to refuse to project or plan, which would make no sense. This would be even more shocking if it were to contradict a well-anchored tenet of western culture: setting an objective, giving oneself a plan to reach it and trying not to deviate from it. But, in addition to the tunnel vision of the method, the risk, when situations get harder and more complicated is then to push dogmatism until the plan is preferable to the reality. This tendency shows itself regularly because it is so difficult and restrictive to modify or change an objective on which everyone has agreed. It therefore distances itself from Cartesian thinking, which considers, on the contrary, that we must start our thinking with what we know with certainty and to slowly expand the field of study. However, today, we see that fixed end staterely on hypotheses over which the intervening force has little to no leverage. Instead of starting out from the real, meaning the situation in progress, no matter the complexity, it builds its reflection starting from the desired situation for the end of the intervention. The logic which prevails nowadays is paradoxically barely Cartesian, even if it claims this connection.

An Approach that Uses Complexity

We will therefore look for an approach that will allow us to start from the real, as complex as it might be, and the opportunities that present themselves rather than the definition of a distant objective, ambitious but hypothetical; an operation that will reconcile political options and military objectives to return to the terms set forth in General Dempsey's anecdote. Philosopher and sinologist François Julien, through the reflections he proposes in his Traité de l'efficacité provides us with convincing elements that help us envision a kind of strategic thinking that would not focus on a goal to achieve but rather on the way of transforming the real. Why go looking so far for something that was the norm in France just a few decades ago? Why take an interest in this eastern wisdom that westerners approach with as much curiosity as condescendence? Because the Chinese philosopher, notably brought back into fashion by the authors of La guerre hors limites[3] has the benefit of pushing this reasoning to a fever pitch. Not content

3. Qiao Liang and Wang Xiangsui, *La guerre hors limite* (Payot et Rivages, 2003)

with being a war-like mystic, portrayed in bucolic and animal metaphors, he develops a complete philosophy of action, going from theory to practice. He presents, therefore, a radical option whose study allows us to better perceive the discrepancy within today's logic.

Exploiting the Potential of Situations

As we look for efficiency, "rather than raising a model that serves as the norm for its action"[4], the Chinese strategy focuses its attention on the course of things, so that as it evolves, it can discover connections and make use of its changes. This strategy tries to track the favorable factors at work in the premise; thus, instead of attaching a goal to an action, it lets itself be caught up in what is happening; in short, instead of imposing its plan on the world, it will rely on the potential of the situation. Beyond the distance taken in relation to the notion of the plan, it's the notion of the "potential of a situation" which is absolutely central here, one that we must take the time to explore. The idea was developed so that "each situation is by itself a source of effect"[5]; this is therefore the ability to perceive effects and use them as opportunities that will build the mark of a great strategy. To better understand this notion of the potential of the situation, the classic metaphor of a flood is enlightening.

---

4. François Jullien, *Traité de l'efficacité* (Grasset, 1997)
5. *Ibid.*

The flood, in its rush forward,directly carries along the rocks, without any efforts. This natural movement of war relies on two main determiners which are the slope and the narrowness of the bed. Fighting this movement of water seems difficult and dangerous. On the other hand, it's possible, when playing with these determiners, to influence its course and its flow and, ultimately, to modify the journey taken by the rocks that were swept away. This image underlines the fact that the analysis of a situation should allow us to discover its guiding principles, the tendencies against which it would be illusory to want to oppose oneself but which possess, in themselves, a strength that is possible to exploit or influence. What is true for the flood is also true for all other situations. A movement of the crowd, a territorial claim, a political ambition... All of these situations that we encounter, what they raise in economic, political or military spheres, possess more or less potential, meaning a capacity that is more or less strong enough to generate effects, be they positive or negative in our eyes.

Setting out from this notion of the potential of a situation, it seems that "it's less our personal investment, in terms of our efforts and our imposition on the world, that counts now than the objective conditioning resulting from the situation: it's that conditioning that I should exploit, on which I should count; this alone is enough to determine success."[6] Additionally, this strategy discredits a certain kind of heroism which,

---

6. *Ibid.*

very often, is only an abundance of energy desperately aiming to create a situation without potential. "If the conditions are lacking, despite the greatest of efforts, the result if disappointing: as heroic as we may be, we will not make an ear of corn grow in the winter."

Approaching Complexity Ahead of Time

However, the metaphor of the flood allows us to develop other aspects. Changing the course of a river at a later time is extremely difficult and will necessitate significant efforts that might not lead to success. Changing the course of a river ahead of time, as close as possible to its source, is a lot easier and requires a lot less effort. Analyzing through the potentials of a situation encourages us to approach situations through the prism of time. The more I am able to intervene early when I see opportunity or danger, the more able I'll be to sustainably and easily influence. Conversely, this image also pushes us to lucidly admit that after a certain threshold, we might not have the available means to effectively influence the development of a situation. This approach encourages as much audacity as it does caution, through a fair evaluation of capacity. Finally, discretion is also an important aspect of this approach. The choice of discretion and humility is of a strategic order, not a moral one. It means not inviting accusations of interference and hegemony. The goal is to orient or reorient a natural slope that is favorable or not favorable to our interests at a moment where media interest is not yet awoken: this discretion increases freedom of action and our ability to intervene and prepare for local susceptibilities.

Clausewitz versus Sun Tzu?

What can we retain from these few excerpts from the written thoughts of Sun Tzu? Very few things, the more Clausewitzien readers will say, as they note that Chinese authorities have long ago swapped this vision of the world for more direct strategic paradigms, inspired by western thought. Readers less allergic to natural metaphors will maybe not find here the foundations of a new strategic school but will at least receive an important reminder: The debate between the importance of seeking out the ends and the necessity to adapt to the real should not be answered once for all. By definition, the strategy is prey to a double constraint; on one side, it should implement everything to attain the objectives set by politicians, on the other side, it must adapt itself to the reality of the situation: these two forces regularly contradict each other. We can only note that today, our scientific approach towards planning, our desire to act comprehensively as well as the inertia of military deployments tends to make us choose the camp of "complying with the plans", to the detriment, very often, of adapting to the real.

The Contribution of General Beaufre

General Beaufre felt the central importance of this question, which he expressed in these terms: "Is it not useless, and even dangerous, to want to assign oneself a future goal? Wouldn't it be better, according to the current practice, to operate at each moment by grounding oneself solely in the events of the moment?"[7] To this question, he provides a very clear answer: "Without global and distant perspectives, action proves sterile. The ends give value to action. Hence the priceless importance of key ideas that define goals without ambiguity. [...] The creation of ideas is very important, it's the source of everything."[8] General Beaufre's decisive contribution does not lie in this response, which is a classic one. His essential contribution comes precisely from the fact that, in refusing to divide the debate between supporters of pragmatic action on one side and "intellectuals wanting to shape the future from ideas"[9] on the other, he offers the roots of a method that aims to "reach the long-term goal, despite the difficulties resulting from the twists and turns of the short term"[10]. But far from considering what he calls the "twists and turns of the short term"[11]

7. General André Beaufre, *Introduction à la stratégie*, coll. « Pluriel » (Hachette, 1998 [re. ed.])

8. General André Beaufre, *Bâtir l'avenir*, coll. « Questions d'actualité » (Calmann Lévy, 1967)

9. *Ibid.*

10. *Ibid.*

11. *Ibid.*

to be simple constraints, he makes it one of the main issues of his method. The obsession of strategy should be to detect events that are bringers of disruption in order to then be able to act on them, either to amplify their range if the events in question are favorable to the "distant goal" or to minimize their consequences if the events considered are harmful to our objectives. As is often the case when it comes to innovation, the issue consists less of inventing revolutionary concepts than of "completing the rejuvenation and rebirth of the eternal strategy"[12]. In order to escape the straitjacket of the comprehensive approach and to offer thoughts that will help us maximize the efficiency of our interventions, it seems especially enlightening to take certain thoughts from General Beaufre and adapt them to the circumstances of today's world. These thoughts will allow us to extract some criteria of efficiency, in order to slightly reduce the fatalism that prevails today when considering the weak output of our military interventions.

Political Diagnosis and Formulation of Political Objectives

We will not attempt to summarize the detailed thinking that General Beaufre has devoted to the expression of political intent. We will simply try to underline all of the visible relevance, lending a certain temporal profundity to political intent. Far from contenting ourselves with

12. General André Beaufre, Introduction à la stratégie, *op. cit.*

providing only end states in each crisis for example, General Beaufre campaigns for the expression of political intent in a wider temporal perspective, allying itself with a series of objectives; he calls this a "political line"[13]. He distinguishes "distant" political objectives from "medium and short term" political objectives. Firstly, the "distant political objectives" are defined by a "distant political diagnosis". All actions must next be put in the order of these "distant goals", without it being possible to directly attain them, since the contingent character of the course of things makes it so that we are permanently obliged to come to terms with the events that arise. As such, "medium and short term political diagnoses" defining short and medium term political objectives, should allow for the orienting of our actions across the "twists and turns" encountered. The interest of this hierarchy-making is that it allows for the implementation of a true "total strategy"[14], which does not limit itself to a series of military responses to successive crises. Without this way of thinking about our actions in the system, there is a great risk that in these periods of "peace-war", threats that were considered in isolation will not take into account the coherence of the politics being carried out and will therefore not provoke enough of an awareness on the part of the population. To this

13. General André Beaufre, *Bâtir l'avenir, op. cit.*

14. According to General Beaufre, this "total strategy" is "charged with designing the direction of the total war. Its role is to define the mission itself and the combination of different general, political, economic, diplomatic and military strategies."

point, the necessity of stabilizing the Sahel-Saharan groups remains below the threshold of mobilizing public opinion. This holds true for the security challenge in Libya and Syria. On the contrary, if as General Beaufre proposes, these threats are thought about in a systemic way, and replaced in a larger context like that of the explosion of the African demographic or the fragility of French society, it becomes possible again to come up with a strategy: leading preventative actions to avoid the collapse of the states, playing the card of development where it's still possible or intervening militarily with weak numbers when the crises are still in their initial stages. If strategy is the art "of making force contribute to the attainment of the goals of politics"[15], the definition of objectives in a hierarchy allows us to extend the field of possible interventions, often more in advance and therefore, in a more coherent manner. Finally, this would allow us, when faced with "operations through weariness"[16], led by Islamist jihadists, to not give into the feeling of always reacting in the face of events. Our actions and reactions would therefore be placed in a hierarchy within the much vaster framework of a true strategy, whose duration would be, on the other hand, considerably increased.

By way of illustration, if we speculate that the "distant goal" of France today is the defense of its territorial integrity and its national cohesion, the two main goals

15. General André Beaufre, *Introduction à la stratégie, op. cit.*

16. *Ibid.*

in the medium term could be the remote maintenance of Islamic destabilization and the fight against clandestine immigration; these objectives being, in turn, able to be reproduced in short-term objectives for all political, economic, diplomatic and military actors.

We could very legitimately counter that this work of defining a direction is already the norm, but this direction remains unknown to the greater public. In this hypothesis, we must therefore not be surprised at the lack of support from the population. Additionally, it's of note that the difficulty of expressing a "distant goal" is nothing new. General Beaufre was already lamenting in his time that the "distant goal" was "so clearly defined amongst the Marxists and so vague in the West."[17].

Framework and Events

Although declaring that "the future remains resolutely unpredictable"[18], General Beaufre tried to plant the foundations for a "projected system", by creating a few simple concepts that would aid in improved understanding of the structure of future events. He first of all qualifies the "frame"[19] of the natural course of events: the "strong trend". This frame is interspersed with "crossroads of the futures", kind of like key moments

17. General André Beaufre, *Bâtir l'avenir*, *op. cit.*
18. *Ibid.*
19. *Ibid.*

where events can take on a new direction. At these foreseeable crossroads of the futures, he then brings into opposition the "crises", the "twists and turns" or the "events", short-term and unforeseeable incidents. These few concept names allow us to explain that our aptitude for changing the directions of long-term tendencies (the frame) primarily depends on our ability to manipulate the short term (crossroads, twists and turns and events), with the goal of having come out at the "most favorable or least unfavorable futures", in terms of our objectives. As such, "through a game of hypotheses, conveniently chosen crossroads and a combinatorial study, we can grasp predictable situations, their probable causes and their consequences and as a result, succeed in determining the situations that we can help promote and the situations that we must look to prevent." The foreseeable situations are not the only events that can be manipulated; crises can be too. Crises "can be dangerous if they develop but they can be useful if we know how to exploit them. In effect, the contradictions that they cause, when they are maintained, can lead to a paralysis of antagonistic forces, while a third party will take advantage of an increased freedom of action. We can also conceive of a maneuver founded on the idea of favoring those contradictions which, by their development, can prevent the most dangerous situations or help resolve certain contradictions, even allowing for the attaining of certain objectives."[20]

20. *Ibid.*

This analysis is clarifying, in that it shows that beyond the internal coherence of military interventions (the balance between ambition, the means and the ways), a superior efficiency can be found by making every effort to better target the moments of interventions. For the same number of troops, means and ambitions, the yields of our interventions can be increased if we try to concentrate our actions on the moments where history is in movement, instead of throwing ourselves into more structural operations, aiming directly to act within the frame. Very concretely, in the French zone of influence, especially in Africa, the strikes of the state and the revolts are "privileged" moments, fleeting moments where the intervention of a third-party country is often wished for by at least one of the warring countries, allowing for the launch into seemingly delicate armed negotiations. The call for help from Malian authorities in December 2012 was doubtless something we could not let pass. We seized the opportunity but we could not fully exploit it. In the last part of our essay, we will offer a few suggested ways of thinking that might help us better seize these events in the future. But before posing the delicate question of "how", the main challenge is to appreciate what General Beaufre calls the "political meaning"[21] of the event and its "disruptive importance". We find here the analysis of the "potential of a situation" from Sun Tzu. All situations are not the

21. In an anecdote, Beaufre emphasizes that Russians make a distinction between "progressive" and "anti-progressive" events.

same. Certain carry only a limited inherent potential; a military intervention, to help or change the direction of a situation, will seem in this case like a strike of the sword in water. Other situations, because they allow for the direct attack of "contradictions" at the origins of crises, permit the rapid development of situations that are more in balance with our objectives.

The Spirit of Geometry and the Spirit of Finesse

A last analysis from General Beaufre is striking in its relevance and its topicality within the framework of an analysis of the efficiency of our operations. It involves reflecting on the position that method should occupy, or "the spirit of geometry", when faced with intuition, "the spirit of finesse"[22].

General Beaufre is, naturally, in favor of the principle of a method. He describes his work as an "attempt to introduce the maximum of rationality to the moving reality of politics"[23]. He justifies his enterprise by noting that the exponential increase in deadliness, notably a consequence of the appearance of atomic weapons, must push us to reduce, as much as possible, the space left for the arbitrary. For all that, he does not succumb to the "forecasting" temptation; the future not leaving

22. Naturally, this is a reference to *Pensées* by Blaise Pascal. In any case, General Beaufre redirects its exact meaning.
23. *Ibid.*

room to "be shut up in a system of predictions because there exist too many potential factors". We have seen it, the only logical attitude that results "consisting not of guessing the future but of methodically building through successive actions, designed in anticipation of promoting the possible futures that we want and to prevent the creations of those possible futures that we fear"[24]. It does not involve restraining "the spirit of finesse" but of "controlling the value of intuitions and even of making emerge new intuitions" through the use of an adapted method. We have previously underlined the dangerous effects of systematically going back to an effects-based approach. This approach, especially relevant in certain cases, like the planning of a campaign of aerial strikes, excessively complicates the process of reflection when it involves thinking of land interventions within populations. Instead of "highlighting the complex mechanisms and interdependences that must be manipulated"[25], instead of concentrating on the seizing of opportunities, on the definition of lines not to be crossed and the reactive adaptation to contingencies, the effects-based approach focuses itself on an imagined goal and integrates it into a structure that is understandable only to initiated peoples.

This assessment, far from being consensual, is notably shared by General Mattis, current United States Secretary of Defense, for whom effects-based operations

24. *Ibid.*
25. *Ibid.*

seem, according to his own terms, like an "intellectual Maginot Line". In 2008, he wrote a directive aimed at abandoning this approach that generated internal friction and was ultimately, counter-productive. One of his conclusions was formulated in this way: "The best way forward is to re-baseline our terminology and concepts by returning to time-honored principles, such as mission type orders, unambiguous commander's intent, and clear articulation of ends, ways and means that have been tested in combat and are historically grounded in the fundamental nature of war while incorporating, where logical, the issues introduced by today's more complex environment."

A simple "message in a bottle" within the framework of this work, we are convinced that the capacity of the general staff, French and allied, to find a good level of balance between "geometric construction" and "the intuitive mind" will be more than ever decisive for the effectiveness of our future engagements.

*

Let us take the time to look at the progress of the development of our analysis. After having defined the efficiency of an intervention, we tried to extensively describe the feeling of inefficiency that might be experienced by the different actors in interventions. We have next offered a critique of certain "fashionable concepts": from the comprehensive approach first, which, in an unfounded way, has nearly been lifted to the rank of strategy; next, other solutions and adaptations that the strategic community has offered and which are equally disappointing. This third part that just ended aimed to provide a rough definition for what could be the principles of a new approach. In order to do this, we have left what we estimated to be the stumbling block of all actions carried out today: the management of complexity, both external (that of the modern world) and internal (that of our own devices). A re-reading of the timeless principles of strategy allows us to extricate two major attitudes in the face of complexity. The first, deeply anchored in the western tradition, consists of taking political ends as the only frame of reference. If this conceptually allows us to never deviate from the motive of the action, it sometimes clashes with a tendency to let adherence to the plans take precedence over reality, even when the defined objectives are unattainable. The second attitude, notably developed in traditional Chinese strategy, tends to favor a reactive adaptation to the real. These two tendencies have their advantages. It's finally General Beaufre who will give us the key to our examination. Far from choosing a "side" in this debate, certainly theoretical, but with very real consequences, he reminds us over the course of his work that this double constraint, between the attaining of objectives and adaptation to the real, is of the same nature as all strategic thought. It even represents its principle challenge. Thus, our collective entitlement to "make force contribute to the attaining of political goals"[26] does not rely so much on the discovery of a new approach which, like a magic formula, would come to solve the impasse in which interventions sometimes find themselves plunged; instead, it lies first and foremost in our ability to adapt ourselves to the situation without ever losing sight of the political objectives in perpetual development. How do we implement this common approach? In all likelihood, through a common strategic culture between the large entities of the state, so that the means and routes to attain objectives are in constant agreement with their development, with none of the "internal frictions" shattering the coherence that must prevail.

We could therefore launch ourselves into the slippery terrain of vain wishes, in hoping that our civil elites, notably those coming from prestigious school, will move back into the field of study of strategy. Does it make any sense that the National School of Administration's (Ecole Nationale d'Administration or ENA) schooling devotes such a small part of its program to issues of defense? Is it not surprising that "studies on war and strategy do not benefit from the institutional and scientific recognition that they're given in other countries"[27]? We could also underline the importance of pursuing and increasing the cultural integration of officers in the civilian world. All of these issues are well

26. General André Beaufre, *Introduction à la stratégie, op. cit.*

27. General Benoît Durieu, *Dictionnaire de la guerre et de la paix* (PUF, 2017) – in the foreword

known. Although certainly there are tracks that could sustainably increase the coherence of our strategies, and thus of our interventions, the object of this essay is not to develop those.

Increasing Efficiency Today

Short term growth of the efficiency of interventions can be attained in different ways. As we emphasized before, it is possible to be more efficient, meaning, to better adhere to political ambition, while trying to better exploit events. To that end, we will now strive to show the importance of looking at our interventions as "armed mediations". We will also raise the delicate question of the political piloting of these interventions, where coordination between diplomatic and military action appears in a new light. This will mean evoking what may seem like a recurring issue: the question of embodiment, at the bottom, of political will. In the end, we will describe the military arrangement needed to successfully complete a long-term strategy, conceived as a succession of limited interventions.

I.

Armed Mediation

Critical Analysis of Operations Serval and Barkhane

In order to anchor our remarks in current interventions, we will begin by highlighting certain aspects of the majority of our interventions in Africa, through the recent example of Operation Serval.

Without going into too much detail, let us simply recall the genesis and broad outlines of this operation. At the end of 2012, Malian authorities asked France for help. After having allowed the eternal identity quest of the Touareg people to crystallize into a jihadist rebellion in the north of the country, authorities in Bamako found themselves incapable of stopping the columns of rebels who threatened to seize the capital. Faced with the risk of seeing installed there a jihadist sanctuary in its zone of influence, and after having been assured that they would receive a UN mandate (resolution 2085 from December 2012), France intervened starting from January 11, 2013. In less than three weeks, more than 5000 men, 1,700 vehicles and 50 aircraft halted the rebels and then brought the fight to the refugee zones in the north of the country. And so, on May 1, 2013, the armed terrorist groups' (GAT) ability to harm was considered sustainably reduced, which meant Bamako could find a certain peace. The rest of the story is known and has been the object of long discussion in the first chapters. What criticisms could we bring in the face of this assessment, which does our armies proud? What remains debatable is whether we gave too complete a victory to the authorities in Bamako. When they presented themselves at the negotiations, aiming to bring a solution to the main origin of the conflict, meaning the question of recognizing the Touareg peoples' identity, they were no longer inclined to make concessions because they had already obtained everything. The lack of willingness on the part of President Ibrahim Abubakar Keita (IBK), still reelected on August 11, 2013 in elections which would have been impossible without the actions of France, would only be confirmed over time. Beyond his refusal to redistribute wealth to the northern part of the country, he pushed provocations, so that some of his close allies in Bamako became the main supporters of the terrorists. He also addressed regular criticisms against France when the occasion presented itself; and thus, the traditional scenario of kicking someone when they're down came to pass. As Patrick Saint-Paul strongly emphasized in a column in the daily newspaper, *Le Figaro*: "France has made mistakes. In the first place, that of having bet on President IBK without a safety net. Paris gives the impression that it supports his corrupt and decaying power, undermining the support of the French presence."[1] Today, the political situation in Mali is at an impasse: the president has neither the capacity nor the desire to take on the immense challenges of his country. French forces are caught between a rock and a hard place: France is a prisoner of its own too emphatic support of a corrupt power. In short, a solution of lies and subterfuge, from which it seems difficult to come out the winner.

Operation Serval seems paradoxically to have been too fast; it obtained tactical successes at the wrong time, diplomatically. Diplomatic power literally arrived "after the war". Since the diplomatic time didn't coincide with the time of the operations, diplomacy was robbed of one of the main levers it possessed on the part of the warring party that solicited its help: the use of constraint. Malian power was no longer in the necessary position to put an end to the marginalization of the opponent, namely the Touareg people; it is even less likely to lead a constitutional reform that aims to share the power or, at minimum, provide improved recognition. As we underlined in the first part of the paper, the "intervention-stabilization-normalization" continuum of operations, because it generates a perfect disruption of the ecosystem in which it is implemented, is a dangerous blueprint and not very effective in this kind of conflict: conflicts which involve, above all, the

1. Patrick Saint-Paul, « Gagner la paix au Mali », *Le Figaro*, January 29, 2018

dissuading of two opponents from resorting to violence in order to settle their differences.

Approach Through Mediation

Could this fatal chain of events be avoided? Maybe, if we had looked at our intervention like a mediation. Since it involved, above all, the restoring of balance between two warring groups who seemed sentenced to living together, the parallel to a mediation imposes itself, with two fundamental nuances: the good offices of the mediator were only immediately recognized by one of the parties and the mediator wasn't in a position of neutrality, since it possessed a task force to weigh in on the course of things. Otherwise stated, the approach that we propose, very much inspired by certain mediation theories, aims to change our way of considering the interventions that we carry out, usually in reaction to political-humanitarian catastrophes. Far from imposing a political structure that conforms to the western model, the intervention must be thought of as a mean to channel the process of the country's political maturation even as this process "surges forward" and threatens France's interests. This means, as President Macron has expressed on several occasions, more effectively linking interventions with the diplomatic roadmap. In this framework, the intervention does not claim to be a political solution but only a decisive step forward in the diplomatic process.

In the case of Mali, this strategy could have been implemented in the following way. Before the intervention, a first phase of negotiations would have been necessary to settle with the Malian president what France expected from the intervention it was planning. These compensations could have notably included a public commitment from the Malian president.[2] This would have meant that within a few months, he would have committed himself to putting into place a better ethnic representative in the state apparatus, as is the case in Niger or Nigeria. This politics of "extending the hand of friendship" before the start of the hostilities aims to create the conditions that will defuse ethnic conflict. The announcement of the Malian president would certainly not have been enough to put an end to the age-old defiance of the Touareg tribes towards the authorities in Bamako, but it would have allowed him to show the more moderate elements of the Touareg side that a negotiated outcome was still possible. What is looked for is the carrying out of a strong, symbolic act, considered unthinkable by the rebels, which shows oppressed ethnic groups that their situation could finally develop favorably. It means treating what some theoreticians call the "cultural trauma"[3] that underpins the conflict or breaking the "psychological dynamism"[4] that rebels

2. The ubiquity of the media, often considered a constraint, here turns out to be an asset.

3. Dean G. Pruitt, "The Theory of Haste: a Reformulation of the Theory of Maturity", Cairn.info.

4. *Ibid.*

"pull from their frustration"[5] by splitting them into multiple camps. On one side, there are those who agree to enter into a process of negotiation and renounce violence; on the other, those who remain on the path of rebellion. Without this prerequisite, the intervening force condemns itself to having to face an enemy that is determined because it is cornered.

The second phase of this strategy relates to the effective deployments of troops. It depends on the "exchanges" obtained during the preliminary phase of negotiations. If the Malian president had consented to the politics of "extending the hand of friendship" towards the Touareg people, a deployment up until the loop of Niger would have allowed them to interrupt the progress of the Touareg rebels, without giving the impression to authorities in Bamako that France had unreservedly committed itself to staying through the crisis settlement, up until it had finally ended. If the Malian president had refused the "extended hand of friendship", a minimal deployment around Bamako to protect our citizens would have then been implemented. In both cases, it would mean maintaining the two sides in what Zartman calls "a mutually painful impasse"[6]. The objective would be to put pressure on Bamako by letting it know that the support of France would require the ending of political marginalizing of the minorities in the North, namely the Touareg people. On their

5. *Ibid.*
6. *Ibid.*

side, the rebels would have to understand that their legitimate reasons for revolt had been heard but that their claims and illegitimate actions would no longer be tolerated and that they would have to recognize the authority of Bamako on Malian territory. In this way, the intervention would fully play its role of diplomatic leverage, while compelling the parties to make decisions that would be unimaginable without the pressure of a third party. Over the course of this phase, the intense work of negotiation with the Touareg people would be conducted through diplomatic channels (notably the Sahel and Algeria) or through intelligence agencies. It would mean informing the rebels that the alternative is simple: negotiate and obtain the representation that they've been demanding for dozens of years, or pursue rebellion and face Franco-Malian troops.

Logically, the third phase consists of exerting differentiated military and diplomatic pressure on the different actors in order to bring together the different agendas towards an acceptable compromise, either in the form of a treaty or a return to the pre-conflict situation. The actors who "play the game" grow stronger and obtain more guarantees, while those who do not play the game are punished: the rebels who pursue the path of terrorism are neutralized. If it's the authorities in Bamako who do not play the game, military support of the third-party country is reduced, even suspended, until the convincing signs of cooperation appear.

It means "proceeding by successive actions, cut by negotiations"[7]. Presented in a very simplified way, using the Malian example, this method, to be effective, requires a certain number of criteria for success to be achieved.

Legitimacy

The first criterion is that of legitimacy. Along with traditional international legitimacy (a UN mandate), which is necessary from the point of view of the law, legitimacy in the eyes of the warring nations must be sought. Without this, all force will be perceived as pure western interference, when it must be seen as a response to a local demand. To be able to influence the course of matters, without risking the phenomenon of rejection, the intervention should be seen as a reaction to a call rather than unilateral action.

Additionally, the neutrality that is systematically displayed to anchor our legitimacy is often counterproductive. Our African partners, often questioned on this subject, would much rather hear that France is intervening to protect its citizens, to guarantee its supply of uranium or to reduce the instability of groups in the Sahel-Saharan region, in the hopes of reducing the flow of immigrants towards Europe, rather than that we are disinterested or that we're intervening in the name of moral principles. As we have explained in the first

7. General André Beaufre, *Introduction à la stratégie*, *op. cit.*

part, the ghosts of neocolonialism are far from buried. A reason for intervention that stated "we are securing Africa so that Africans can live on their continent" would provoke debates in France but would be very well received on the other side of the Mediterranean.

Spotlighting Weak Ambition

The second criterion that we identify is linked to the perception of intervention in the media.

In the few days that mark the start of an intervention, we have seen the very classic move of over-communicating the decisive role played by France and its armies. This attitude, which can seem natural and legitimate, tends to create an expectation which will then be difficult to fulfill.

It would be a mistake however to imagine that we could lead an intervention, involving a full task force, without communicating. War "below the media threshold" can function when it is led by a small corps, with a light logistical imprint; this is notably the case for special and underground combat. This discretion is, on the other hand, difficult to envisage when a task force is engaged. In this case, only a strategy that aims to minimize the scale of the intervention allows for the preservation of the freedom of political maneuver. In this way, when dealing with an "armed mediation", it's crucial to hammer home the point in the media that France is intervening at the request of a third party, that its action is looking to prevent an explosion of violence, that it is not looking to create a state nor administrations, that the political solution can only come from the warring nations themselves, that democracy can only be the fruit of a long process of political maturation, etc. In these conditions, the executive government's freedom of action is preserved, an exit door being left permanently ajar. Depending on how events develop, all options of withdrawal remain possible. If the armed mediation is a success, the withdrawal can begin as soon as the peace agreement is signed; if no peace agreement seems imminent, a swift and brutal withdrawal (without any bridging operations) remains possible; the refusal of a structuralist approach remaining always the line that must not be crossed. We would have to wait to be solicited again if the situation degenerates. This new request, because it would be seen in perspective with the first intervention, would allow us to exert an even stronger pressure on the warring countries within the framework of a new armed mediation.

Discretion

The third key factor is discretion. As we have just explained, this does not mean looking to hide our actions: we do not conceal the action of a task force. The discretion that we seek from our commitments concerns the diplomatic work, the work of putting local actors under pressure. Two main reasons demand this discretion.

The first finds its origin in the necessity of keeping a blurred line around France's actions and those of local actors. If the France's actions are too easily "figured out", the French political project is too easily associated with pure interference; rejection then becomes easies as soon as the first difficulties are encountered. Conversely, if France's actions, without being secret, maintain their blurred outlines, local actors find it more difficult to discern what results from French pressure and what results from local will. Without being denied, France's actions, to be effective, should be able to get lost in the embroilment of the situation.

The second reason for discretion with regards to France's actions is the necessity of caution when it comes to the images of the authorities on which we will exert pressure. The images of the presidents of countries in which we intervene should be respected at all costs, at the risk of undermining their future ability to govern; no matter what the conditions of their elections, they represent their people and their country. If we allow ourselves an analogy with the analysis of Ernst Kantorowicz in *The King's Two Bodies*, the "mystical body" of the authorities that we compel must be protected while the "mortal body" might be the object of negotiations and discreet pressures. This remark on the necessity of the secret in mediation is a commonplace of diplomacy. There is nonetheless a certain French habit to "lecture" that has developed over these last few years, making our messages less acceptable. What is valid for the highest level of the state is equally true for all authorities holding a morsel of power.

"Analytical Empathy"[8]

A fourth criterion for success can be found in our ability to figure out the motives of the different warring nations with which we will be interacting within the framework of a negotiation. It's crucial to not too quickly succumb to the siren calls of simplification by putting warring nations into one of three categories: friends, enemies and those who are neutral. By demonstrating a certain "analytical empathy", theoreticians of mediation demonstrate the relevance of attempting to understand the deep motives of warring nations. If we accept that there can be legitimate motives in certain groups who resort to illegitimate actions (even in the case of terrorism), our analyses are certainly less neat but our ability to help a political solution emerge increases accordingly. These remarks might be shocking, especially in an era where we refuse any form of otherness for our enemies, but they're not new. They belong to the tradition of General Poirier, who already highlighted the limits of the friend-enemy dialectic in limited conflicts, and who himself preferred the Same-Other[9] dialectic. They can

8. Dean G. Pruitt, *op. cit.*

9. General Lucien Poirier, « Stratégie intégrale et guerre limitée », *Stratégique*, no. 54, February 1992

also be found in the work of René Girard who in Achever Clausewitz explains that one of the worst pitfalls in conflict settlement is to deny the humanity of the other.

Political Steering

The second to last criterion of success that we want to evoke is, in all likelihood, the most central and will be the object of a longer development in the following chapter. For an armed mediation to be able to see the light of day, it's imperative that a political steering, going far beyond simple political control, be implemented. In fact, since this involves the daily exerting of pressure on certain actors, adapting the use of force, seizing opportunities, implementing a true political engineering, changing order which from one day to the next become obsolete in the face of shifts within the warning nations, political steering assumes an essential nature. It cannot limit itself to a coordination coming from the "place of Paris". The question of decentralizing the decision and the subsidiarity must be asked. We will return to this.

Pre-positioning and Reactivity

The last criterion for success is linked to the way in which armed forces are used. For an armed mediation to have a chance at success, it must know how to play on the full scale of regular and irregular combat, "paired" war and special and clandestine combat.

A quick look at specific cases will allow us to better understand the principles developed up until now. Let's take the example of an event, announced long ago: the succession of President Déby. There is a strong probability that Chad, familiar with a new period of keen tensions, could go to civil war if the Sudanese or Toubou rebels manage to structure their actions. Given France's interests there and the long tradition of cooperation that unites these two countries, the possibility of an intervention cannot be dismissed. If this last is led according to current aims, there is a great risk of stalemate and discredit; discredit as much in the eyes of the "dauphin" as the protestors or international opinion. On the contrary, if this last point is considered more astutely, skillfully combining military and diplomatic actions, there's the possibility of achieving a solution, albeit one that is far from being perfect and acceptable to everyone.

What we have developed under the title of "armed mediation" is not new in terms of strategy or diplomacy. It involves an adaptation of diplomacy to the context of current operations. This method is close to the realist school of international relations, in the central place it gives to power and the states; it is "Aronien" in its willingness to take into account the deep forces of metapolitical data. Certain readers will see here a return to Realpolitik, even of Françafrique. We, however, are convinced that our way of thinking of interventionism is more respectful to the rights of the peoples in African states. It recognizes their sovereignty in what concerns their political maturation, without being naïve enough to think that a policy of laisser-faire would be compatible with French interests.

In proposing that we revisit the coordination between diplomatic and military actions through organizational adaptations, the strategy of armed mediation aims to put an end to what General Desportes calls, in a slightly abrupt way, "our pathetic inability to integrate and coordinate our diplomatic and military actions each time we try to put an end to war". To become operational, this reflection would merit further developments. This new way of thinking about our interventions is, we've just seen, conditioned by the development of two capacities: firstly, a more reactive political steering of interventions; next, the putting in place and the support of a military arrangement that allows for the exerting of differentiated military pressures on different warring nations.

2.

The Embodiment of Political Will

When a feeling of inefficiency emerges, no matter whether within the framework of an external intervention or in the vaster one of leading public politics, one of the invariable responses is that we should designate an authority whose mission will be to ensure that "the will of the Prince" is properly interpreted, without being betrayed in his implementation. The authorization of such a person makes them, of course, the object of debates. Certain can only imagine him in a role of control, aiming to ensure the right balance between political ambition and actions that are concretely carried out; others consider that beyond control, they should ensure the correct coordination amongst different actors, both civil and military, in the intervention; finally, the last group think that they should have levers available to them that will guarantee this efficiency and incite the sought-after balance. Since we are on a quest for concrete actions that will be able to gain margins of efficiency, it seems like an interesting idea to weigh the relevance of this embodiment of political will, in order to try to pin down its outline and its main limits.

A Few Historical Examples

Without launching into a long history, it's of note that this issue is an ancient one. In a way, the use of the missi dominici by the last Merovingian kings, then by the Carolingian kings came from a commitment to effectively pass on royal authority in reassuring themselves that the decisions made would be correctly understood and applied, despite the different "frictions" which could diminish it, starting with distance. The examples of what we call today the decentralization of power are numerous. We will focus on the case that best corresponds to what we are looking to study: a short-term embodiment of political will at the time of an armed conflict.

Unsurprisingly, the colonial period is filled with examples. From Bugeaud and de Lattre to Lyautey, all of these marshals saw themselves entrusted, using different titles, with powers at once military and civilian; Resident-General for Lyautey in Morocco, Governor-General for Bugeaud in Algeria, High Commissioner, Commander-in-Chief for de Lattre in Indochina. The option of entrusting civil and military responsibilities to the same person appeared necessary for several reasons, which were not limited to the distance of theaters of operation and the difficulties of communication.

In order to successfully complete the wars of conquest and pacification that were necessary for the colonial project, it seemed obvious that the leader had to hold concurrently civil and military functions: it was the only way to gather all the levers of control into one hand in order to ensure success, quickly react and base their authority close to their representatives. Naturally, times changed and today, we can imagine only with difficulty a military with so much power. To that end, the example of Jacques Soustelle, Governor-General of Algeria from 1955 to 1956, is very interesting, even if he is seen as an exception. Pierre Mendès France chose Soustelle a man of left-leaning politics and an ethnologist by training, to solve the Algerian crisis. By doing so, Mendès France broke with the habit of only naming military men to these "proconsul" posts. There exists therefore a precedent of a senior official performing this function.

The embodiment of political ambition is not an exclusively French issue. The British, over the course of their long colonial experience, have also tested out numerous ways to embody political power during times of war. The politico-military organization chosen against the insurrection in Malaysia at the start of the 1950s is often seen as an example: in addition to embodying political will through a high commissioner, tasked with coordinating the actions of security forces and the administration, a whole system of civilian-military committees, organized in a network across the entirety of Malaysia was created[1]. The political embodiment in this case is passed on through a chain and does not therefore lie with one man. Still taking inspiration from the British, we could of course find in the figure of Winston Churchill an illustration of the necessity of uniting power in one person, in order to be assured of operational coherence. To those who criticized his willingness to hold at the same time the powers of Prime Minister and Minister of Defense, he explained: "It's essential to have at the head a single will that exerts a hold over the entirety of the field of action, loyally assisted and corrected of course, but whose authority is maintained in its integrity."[2] This quote, which describes the need for coherence at the highest levels of the state remains an interesting argument when these principles are seen at the scale of an intervention. The person of Churchill, the nightmare of the highest ranked among his military subordinates, is doubtless too colorful a character to serve as a model; an excerpt from a letter from his son, Randolph Churchill, member of the British expeditionary force in Cairo in 1941, expresses this need for political embodiment in the theater of operations: "I do not see how we can start to win the war here, as we don't have here a competent civilian to give us, from day to day, a political and strategic direction to follow.

1. Jennifer Dybman, « Les opérations d'influence britanniques de l'empire à l'Afghanistan », *Intelligence on line*, no. 714 and no. 798 ; *DSI*, no. 134, March-April, 2018

2. Winston Churchill, *The Second World War* (coll. « Texto », Tallandier, 2013, volume 2)

Why not send a member of the War Cabinet to preside over all war efforts? [...] Most of the thinking people here realize the necessity of a radical reform, with precisely this in mind."[3]

A Current Need

We could, of course, think that this idea of embodied political power in the theaters of operation is a reflex of the past. Thanks to technological progress, especially in communication, what would have been in yesteryear decided locally can today, almost in real time, be decided in the policy centers closest to power. In addition, given the sensitivity of missions and the media consequences that actions on the ground can have, we can understand the hesitance about delegating to a third party, no matter how competent, a responsibility as politically sensitive as the conducting of a war.

And yet, there are many reasons that might lead us to believe in the continued relevance of the embodiment of political ambition in current theaters of intervention. The first reason is perfectly described in the Senate's information report on the assessment of external operations on July 13, 2016: faced with the abundance of actors close to the crisis countries, the great difficulty of coordination between different interveners and the necessity of building coherent solutions that were acceptable to

3. *Ibid.*

local authorities, the coordination efforts that were agreed upon in Paris were not enough to maintain the coherence of action of "the French team". Daily political management, even led locally by a special representative in the theater of war is necessary for the presidential will to not be betrayed by the frictions of its implementation, no matter their origins. It's of note that general officers who have recently led interventions regularly make this same observation[4]. It is paradoxical to ceaselessly repeat that "solutions will not only be military ones", while at the same time, not designating a local arbitrator who knows how to use and coordinate the levers of security, governance and development, depending on the circumstances. It is equally paradoxical to think that the military alone can take into account all of the different parts of an intervention.

A second reason justifying the need for an embodiment of presidential will in the theaters of intervention lies in the difficulty of maintaining a consistent relationship and exerting pressure on partners with whom a cooperation is being established. Today, the heads of state of five countries making up G5 Sahel deal with five ambassadors, multiple special representatives and the head of the Barkhane forces[5]. This abundance of

4. The final reports of the different mission are naturally, classified. The remarks noted within the framework of this study have been gathered from conferences held at the École de guerre.

5. With Jean-Marc Chataigner, France has certainly sent "an emissary of France to the Sahel". Chataigner's rights do not seem to extend to being allowed to embody French political ambition.

representatives tends to produce a dilution of responsibilities and maintains a blurriness that is harmful to the coherence of the operation. If, today, a partner does not honor the commitments taken during the meeting between heads of state, it risks only, in the short term, a polite reminder from the diplomatic command. The presence of a single representative of power, whose authority is recognized, having at hand the real levers of control, notably military and financial, would fundamentally allow for immediate reactions and even better anticipation. This would simplify relations and allow for a faster and more direct steering that would be more susceptible to reduce the occurrence of tense situations, or even the "kicking of someone when they're down". This embodiment of political power on the ground would allow for, in short, the leading of the kind of armed mediation presented in the previous chapter.

Finally, the classic argument that technological progress will allow for the real-time steering of operations from Paris cannot stand in light of the reality of situations. Far from favoring subsidiarity, the current means of communication are paradoxically reinforced by the tendency towards centralism. The decision-making autonomy of the ground levels continues to diminish, giving the impression, little by little, that all decisions are made in Paris. This situation tends to lengthen the time it takes to carry out the completion of concrete actions.

At this stage of our reflection, one question is essential. If the decentralized embodiment of political ambition seems to be, as we maintain, a need often mentioned, why has it not seen the light of day? And when it does, why is it in a form that is too toned down to be effective?

Reluctances for its Implementation

If the apparent necessity to embody political ambition remains at a dead end, it's because it infers a certain number of consequences which seem to eclipse the hypothetical margins of efficiency it would allow. Without being exhaustive, two main consequences must be highlighted.

The first consequence could lead to true institutional disruption. For the actors on the ground, the arrival of a high commissioner, dubbed by the president of the Republic, would inevitably be synonymous with the loss of freedom of action since this commissioner would become the unquestionable leader of the intervention. For everyone, militaries and diplomats, this would inevitably involve a thorough review of respective rights. Many would surely be ready to agree to this if the benefits in terms of efficiency were certain; but there is an equally high risk that a new actor will only add another layer of complexity to an already complicated situation. The few recent experiences[6] in this

6. We might think of the role of Bernard Kouchner, senior representative of the UN from 1999 to 2001, or that of Paul Bremer, administrator of Iraq in 2003.

area are not always reassuring. The overhaul of rights, far from limiting itself to actors on the ground would also affect institutions in Paris. Ministers' freedom of actions would be constrained, that of the Military Chief of Staff could also see its rights as leader of operations quite reduced. In short, the appointing of a "senior representative", far from being a secondary concern, inevitably implicates major upheavals on an institutional scale. The second consequence is that giving politico-military powers to one person means choosing a leader. For militaries, there is no doubt that this person must be the Commanding General of the forces, the armies being, in general, the "majority shareholder" in interventions. Beyond the technical nature of the role of being military commander, leading an expeditionary force is not an improvisational exercise; the general staff is today designed to always integrate other elements. The integration of a pillar of development and a political advisor of the highest level would technically pose not a single difficulty. For the armies, military arrangements are naturally designed to make up the head and the backbone of interdepartmental action on the ground. For the other departments, the militaries' arguments, while based in common sense, would be seen as contradicting the idea that "the sword must give way to the toga", a reminder from the time of the Algerian War that illustrates the consequences of too large a place being granted to generals.

Beyond the problems of the "schools of thoughts", the choice of a political leader poses questions about personality and personal abilities. Who could well be this "rare bird" who must, at the same time, have the intimate trust of the president of the Republic, be a perfect diplomat and master the use of armed forces? If in the place of a Kissinger, the political management of an intervention was seen to be entrusted to a young, brilliant civil servant, whose only asset is that he has walked along the same prestigious hallways as the president, the merging of politico-military powers into the hands of one person could quickly turn into a disaster.

Embodiment: Rising to the Challenge

In the end, if there is a great temptation to see in political embodiment a recipe for increasing the coherence of interventions, the risks of such a method should not be underestimated. Must we, in light of these risks, throw it into the graveyard of not-so-good ideas? We don't think so. A quick look at military history shows that successes are almost always obtained through technological or organizational innovations. Within the framework of limited conflicts, over the course of which success is synonymous with coherence, rethinking the place of the political leader of interventions makes sense.

To be operational, the embodiment of political will should therefore be astutely evaluated. Before anything else, it would be convenient to think of this in institutional terms. A senior representative with neither status nor budget, having only the trust of the president, would in all likelihood be "absorbed" by the large system, as are many of the high commissioners who are today implicated in conflict settlements. On the other hand, a high commissioner, leaving aside his own abilities, if he is named to the Council of Ministers[7], if he can be present at defense councils, if his connection with the Military Chief of Staff is developed and if he is shown to be entrusted with a budget, would perhaps be more able to directly exercise his double role of coordinating actors and exerting pressure on warning nations. If the idea of appointing him a general staff would doubtless be an error (the objective is not to create an additional decision-making level), the idea of reinforcing his role with a few important subordinates, in order to create a chain of control and political guidelines on the English model in Malaysia would be worth studying, notably within the framework of armed mediation.

After the question of status, that of the right person is fundamental. The "job description" might intimidate, since it involves finding a recognized personality, having the total trust of the president, being experienced enough to be able to free yourself from the influence of systems, being a specialist in the mysterious workings of the diplomatic-military field and being committed to neoclassical realism without, for all that, being a war hawk... In short, it involves, in a way, finding the

---

7. This is the main recommendation from the Senate information report previously cited.

"Kissinger" or the "Raymond Aron"[8] from among all the possible candidates. More seriously, rather than wait for a messiah, it would make a lot more sense to buckle down to creating this elite by "politicizing" certain of our best flag officers, or "militarizing" our most warlike diplomats. Perhaps former Heads of the President's Military Chiefs-of-Staff (Chefs de l'état-major particulier du president, CEMP), former Military Chiefs-of-Staff, former ambassadors having operational experience or former heads of intelligence services, newly retired, would be the best candidates, if of course they'd acquired, over the course of exercising their responsibilities, the trust of the president. An order precisely defining the nature of this function and its place in the apparatus of the state would therefore be necessary.

8. Often compared to Henry Kissinger and questioned about the fact that he never held a true role as an actor in international relations, Raymond Aron recognized in his memoirs that with his scruples, he couldn't have been anything other than a commentator. The idea of entrusting the leading of our interventions to experts is to be handled with caution.

3.

Reflection on the Use of Forces

In writing this piece, we have decided to risk formulating a few concrete paths towards increasing the efficiency of our interventions, so as not to remain in the comfortably limited positions of commentators or critics. Since today Operation Barkhane represents an essential part of the external effort of the armies, the last pages of this piece will try to outline what might be the French plan in the Sahel. Far from being disconnected from previous chapters, the adaptations of the plan here offered are examples of what the military tool should be within the armed mediation framework as we have just shown it.

Returning to a Logic of Advance Positioning

Before reflecting on adaptations of the French plan in the Sahel, we must first of all understand the political objectives pursued by France in this region. We have underlined these objectives on multiple occasions in our study, which are only known with certainty by the highest authorities of the state and are anyhow changing. To be able to start our analysis, we will retain as the basis of our reflection the end state of Operation Barkhane, as we see it in the Paris-based general staff. The end stateof Operation Barkhane consists of bringing the terrorist threat to a manageable level for the armies in the sub-region so that they can face it. It concretely results in a double effort: the direct damage to terrorists, meaning the commitment of armed forces to destroying one part of them, and the support of local armies, notably within the frame of the joint force of G5 Sahel (FC-G5S).

Even a basic analysis of the situation in the Sahel would allow us to confirm, with relative certainty, that this will not be able to be attained in the medium or long term. As such, to break the feeling of stalemate that risks, in the short term, of making a dent in political freedom of action, it would be relevant, before anything else, to separate this from a specific operation, like Operation Barkhane today by assigning it, more widely, to a pre-positioned French plan in Africa. It could be useful, owing to the first good results from FC-G5S[1] (as anecdotal as they are) to officially put an end to Operation Barkhane and to return to the situation that has prevailed from decolonization up until Operation Serval: a logic of pre-positioned troops who

1. This refers to the G5 Sahel Joint Force, composed of Mali, Chad, Mauritania, Niger and Burkina Faso (FC-G5S).

remain permanently ready to intervene, in three principle cases: supporting African countries over the course of their long process of political maturation, in order to temper the most serious effects of the crisis; answer to requests from African armies to successfully complete their missions; intervene with very short notice, unilaterally or not, to enforce French interests (with a permanent effort towards the protection of our citizens).

This desire to pass from a logic of operations to a logic of pre-positioning might seem like a game of sleight-of-hand semantics. It is not. If politics is ultimately the only judge of the efficiency of operations, it remains largely dependent on the image that voters and media outlets make of the intervention track record.

However, an operation that is founded on long-term objectives is today regularly written off as being considered a failure. To guard against this tendency, it would make sense to bring together structural, long-term, objectives in our military plan abroad[2] and to give our operations only short-term, militarily attainable objectives. Let's take a last example to anchor our remarks. If tomorrow, G5 Sahel calls upon France to base a patrol on the frontier between Mauritania and Mali from March to April, 2019, it would be relevant to think about this appeal as a fully-fledged operation, with a name, an objective and a specific space and time frame.

---

2. No one has called into question the logic of pre-positioning practiced by all of the powers looking to have regional or global influence.

This sequencing would allow for the giving of a better media clarity to our action and would break this feeling of stalemate by proposing successive achievements, regular successes. This "storytelling", as has become a popular term to use, would better correspond to our media-friendly time, thus making it more understandable and acceptable to the population. It would allow for, as we have said in previous chapters, a return of a strategic meaning to our operations since it would involve, with each request, a return to a dialectic of what is wanted[3], using force as the main lever. The last point here, but certainly not the least, the choice of advance positioning would follow a long period of time, marked by limited groups for operations that would be fundamentally about reducing the efficiency of the battle of attrition led by our enemies[4] because it would prevent the force from settling down for too long a period of time in the same place. This scattering and this reactivity would of course pose a logistical challenge; we will come back to this. After having campaigned for an advance planning logic and defined three main cases of engagement, we will now get on with describing its characteristics.

3. Or, a double dialectic: against the enemy on one side, with our allies on the other.

4. More concretely, the logic of concentration then dispersion greatly reduces forces' IED exposure; no true routine can be operated.

Advance positioning: a few constants

In view of the "specifications" that we have just defined, taking equally into account the considerations developed in the chapter on armed mediation, the pre-positioned French presence which could take over Operation Barkhane should be sharpened so that it can intervene autonomously[5] while also supporting armed partners[6]. It should also be capable of exerting differentiated military pressure on different actors[7]. One sizeable part of the current presence of Operation Barkhane could therefore be maintained, at the cost of a few adjustments.

The operating command could be exercised through the current Joint Command Post of Operation Barkhane in N'Djamena[8], subject to expanding its rights so that it becomes a true regional command post (CP), having the final say about the entirety of the pre-positioned troopsin Gabon, Senegal or Ivory Coast (according to the current layout). No matter the exact position, this regional CP would have to be the sub-regional, politico-military

5. Within the framework of the third case, previously described: "intervening with very short notice, unilaterally or not, to enforce French interests" (notably for the protection of our citizens)

6. This would mean supporting African countries during their long processes of political maturation, in order to temper the effects from the most serious crises and respond to requests from African armies to help them successfully complete their missions.

7. Necessary to be able to lead an armed mediation.

8. This is known by the title, Joint Command Post (*Poste de commandement interarmées de théâtre*: PCIAT)

integrator, a representative on the strategic level, capable of welcoming the political leader of an intervention, the advisors of other ministries, etc. The presence of the air force could remain almost the same, the idea being to find the right balance between the capacity to send and then support the troops everywhere in the Sahel-Saharan strip, without maintaining a too large number of operational areas.

On the other hand, the true challenge consists of rethinking the engagement of the infantry: seemingly irreconcilable choices have to be made.

Pre-positioning of Land Units: Irreconcilable Choices

In an ideal world, the regional presence that we'd want, starting from two or three advance positioning zones (Senegal, Gabon, the Republic of Côte d'Ivoire) would allow for the rapid launching of military detachments in a country where we would like to intervene: either in launching detachments aimed at accompanying partner armies into combat in order to maximize their efficiency through the supplying of key abilities (air-ground support, anti-tank, surface-to-surface support, medical support, intelligence support, support of command, etc.); or in sending entirely French units to, through direct engagement or through pure deterrence, make inescapable the defeat of the enemy; or finally, in using advance support bases, notably to give some leeway to aircraft.

This ideal solution constitutes a true challenge since it seems to disregard the reality of operations. In fact, from a logistical point of view, France, even supported by its partners, does not have the strategic transport capacities to, in a reactive way, engage and disengage armored vehicle units. Some have concluded from this that we must give up on armor-plating. It's a real question that we'll bring up later. For now, let's hold onto the idea that this solution is today politically unrealistic[9], the protection of the lives of soldiers being today a priority. Next, plug and play[10] seems to be a fantasy. To abruptly arrive in a country, mount an operational partnership and then leave to make war, hand in hand, does not work or works badly. There's a minimum of trust and mutual understanding required to go and risk your lives all together. In this way, off-the-ground military presences, that would allow us to "tune in" and then "tune out" at one's leisure, are myths.

For these two main reasons, the current tendency is therefore to settle down (in "FOBs"[11], as they're referred to in military jargon), despite the generally shared conviction that only an improved adaptability of our military presences will allow us to avoid stalemate. All of this then pushes us to believe that our theoretical desire for

---

9. If France was threatened, the question of armor-plating would be a non-issue. Once more, there can only be efficiency here if modes of action are consistent with political will.

10. This is the idea that we could, without significant preparation, cooperate with a discovered local unit.

11. *Forward Operating Bases* (FOB) are American military camps.

advance positioning, armed mediation or "differentiated military pressures" will clash with military contingencies and realities of war. The time of the company of paratroopers, who, through its presence alone or a few gunshots, came to calm African fever seems well and truly over. There is however one solution that exists, in exploiting to their maximum the different times of operating partnerships.

Cooperation to Permit Interaction

One way to overcome these paradoxes is to know how to play on the different kinds of operational military partnerships (OMPs). There exists dozens of ways of helping a partner overcome the security challenges that it might face. Assembled under the term OMP, the methods that make friendly military units effective are the subject of intense reflection in terms of ideology and capacity, both in France and abroad. Units dedicated to this goal are growing more and more visible, especially in the United States[12]. The French infantry is also equipping itself with an OMP leader in order to think about and implement, in the future, more effective partnership actions. Without entering into overly specific considerations, let's keep in mind, for the needs

12. The army has just created its first Security Force Assistance Brigade (SFAB) of around 800 men. Five other SFABs will be ready in about two years, trained in a school devoted to them, called the *Military Advisor Training Academy* (MATA).

of this analysis, that there exist roughly two very different kinds of OMPs.

On one side, there are the actions of the structural OMP, whose most well-known form is cooperation. An approach that is resolutely applied over a long time span, those who are cooperating, some of whom swap their French soldier uniforms for that of the armies which they've come to help, try to advise their counterparts, on a daily basis, to create a more coherent military tool; it's a matter of vey concretely offering management techniques for human and material resources, creating schools, setting up trainings and developing interest for planning. The objective of someone who is cooperating is not to leave for war with the unit that he is advising. His objective is, like a true Sisyphus, to regularly encourage his partner to better structure his defensive tool so that it might be in a position to more effectively realize its missions.

At the polar opposite of this OMP structure, there exists the resolutely short-term actions of the partnership that deal with what we call, following the example of researcher Thomas M. Huber, "compound combat" or "compound warfare"[13]. Far from looking to structure over time a partner so that he might be able to act autonomously, compound combat consists of occasionally making a unit effective by reinforcing it (by "compounding" it) with a detachment that

13. Thomas M. Huber, *Compound Warfare: that Fatal Knot* (General Editor, July 27, 2004)

is capable of implementing the few abilities and key skills that are lacking to prevail over an enemy at a comparable level. The recovery of the cities of Mosul in Iraq and Raqqa in Syria, for example, were achieved through compound combat: a partner, namely Kurdish troops, were clearly reinforced by detachments of western soldiers, who supplied operational capabilities that were of high added value[14] in order to prevail over the soldiers of the Islamic State (IS). In the same way, Russian forces just compounded with Syrian troops in order to take back Aleppo and American and British detachments reinforced Misrati troops to take back Sirte. These experiences of "compound warfare" greatly exceed in their ambition and their modes of action the experience known in Afghanistan, under the name of "Operational Mentoring and Liaison Team" (OMLT): it involved, in Afghanistan, building units of half a dozen people who were integrated into the battalions of the Afghan national army to improve their operational level.

Before concluding this digression into the forms of OMPs and offering an applicable arrangement in the French zone of influence in Africa, it's important to understand that these two forms of OMPs are not mutually exclusive; the two have very different tactical

14. This is not an exhaustive list but the most frequently compounded capacities are the following: observation capacities (drones, ISR), indirect support capacities (shooting, artillery), direct support capacities (anti-tank and long-distance weapons), supply capacities (low-cost digitization, means of transmission), engineering capacities (EOD) and health capacities (relief and care of the wounded).

and political implications, which it would be a good idea to understand. The actions of an OMP that fall under the scope of compound warfare are very effective tactically, with results produced in a few months, sometimes even a few weeks. On the other hand, they sometimes have significant political consequences. The Kurdish example is especially illuminating: the compound aspect allowed for rapid results against the IS. The "Kurdish victory" against the IS has heavy political consequences; the Kurds feel more than ever justified in claiming a higher form of autonomy, to the great displeasure of Turkey. Conversely, the actions of structural OMPs are not so tactically effective in the short term and the political consequences are very often limited. On the other hand, they are the only ones to even produce long-term effects. The ignorance of the tactical abilities and political consequences of the different kinds of OMPs is often at the origin of misunderstandings. Counting on EUTM[15] in Mali to improve the situation in the Sahel-Saharan strip does not make sense in the long term. Counting on any effectiveness from the joint forces of G5S without compound forces seems today fanciful. On the other hand, the different OMP detachments in Operation Barkhane, if they focus on G5S joint forces can obtain convincing results.

The two forms of OMPs that we have just outlined are extremes. The majority of OMP actions make up

15. The European Union Training Mission trains the armies of the different G5 Sahel countries.

a perfect blend of short-term actions and long-term visions. The question then is to know what to emphasize in the French arrangement that we'd like to have in Africa. Today, in the face of political ambition and steady averages, the most relevant kind of arrangement would consist in maintaining, simultaneously, a double network: on one side, a framework for those cooperating in the G5 cities, on the other, pre-deployed French troops, who are ready to be paired.

It would involve, for the network of cooperating troops[16], the setting to work for the achievement of two tasks. First of all, concentrating all our efforts on a partner unit made up of around 300 fighters, in order to be sure that this unit has the means, both human and material, to move securely in the territory. It would not, under any circumstances, mean the creation of an elite unit, equipped with western gear, with too many weapons and people, which would disrupt the delicate ecosystem of local military units[17]. Not focusing on a single unit in particular and looking to form, in turn, a too large a number of units would be another error. Therefore, it involves making sure that the vehicles

16. 5 to 10 cooperating troops per G5 country would be enough. The team example, led by a senior officer (captain) should mainly consist of sub-officers and military at the specialized rank within maintenance.

17. At the moment, the political life of G5 countries seems like a long succession of coups d'état. To counter this tendency, it's vital that no unit goes beyond the rest of the other units. "Praetorian" units (often called the presidential guards) should be capable of playing their role as the *ultima ratio* when faced with the rest of the armies.

and arsenals of the chosen unit exist and that they are suitable for combat; it means seeing what ammunition and fuel can be mobilized, if necessary; it involves helping soldiers reach a minimum level to create a bubble of security around a French military detachment which through the partnering and combination of joint-army means, will locally have the advantage over the enemy. The second task of the cooperating detachment would be to maintain, within the partner unit, a stock of French vehicles and equipment, sufficient without being overabundant[18]. In short, the first objective of those cooperating would be to make sure that, in the five countries that compose G5 (Chad, Niger, Mali, Mauritania and Burkina Faso), France has the "stem units", starting from which it can, when partner countries express their wish for it, lead the action through the partnering of a force.

Alongside this framework of permanent cooperating forces[19], the pre-positioned French presence could revolve around two or three countries. The pre-deployed units for short mandates, of four to six months, should be able to intervene according to different modes: either autonomously, either partnered with other "stem units" from the cooperating force arrangement, or finally, either in a mixed way, accompanied on one side by African units and on the other by entirely French units.

18. One or two warehouses with a dozen armored vehicles between them could be enough.

19. Transfers of two or three years are very possible in the G5 capitals.

The advantages of this kind of arrangement would be numerous. In the short term, the restructuring of units would give the countries in the Sahel, and especially Mali, no choice but to take up their responsibilities. It's reasonable to think that if Operation Barkhane leaves the northern and central areas of Mali, there is a risk that the situation will deteriorate, with MINUSMA[20] finding itself alone on the front lines. At the risk of being cynical, this deterioration is undoubtedly necessary to force the authorities in Bamako out of their inaction and initiate institutional reforms which alone might lay the foundations for a political solution: in short, making them aware of their responsibilities in the face of the seriousness of events. France will then be able to intervene again, this time by leading the war at the pace of political negotiations and retaking the initiative. In the longer term, this new arrangement would allow for the attaining of a fair balance: on one side, it would allow for the defense of our interests and the accompanying of countries in the Sahel-Saharan strip throughout their political maturation process and on the other, it would prevent our country from finding itself embarked upon some kind of structuralist adventure in which armies find themselves inexorably trapped. Additionally, since this arrangement would allow us to more frequently intervene early enough in the settlement of certain crises, without waiting for

---

20. Multidimensional Mission of Nations United for the Stabilization of Mali

the level of catastrophe necessary so that an intervention from France can be started, the volume of engaged forced could be, structurally speaking, smaller.

Are We Ready for This?

Are army land units ready today for compound combat? Do they have a sufficient collection of ideologies and experience to bring about this dramatic change from a traditional organization to an organization that is more tailored to partnering with a foreign force? If a strong empirical experience exists, it has not, at this time, been translated into ideology. Aware of this lack, the Chief of the Land Staff ordered the creation of an OMP command in order to broaden our thinking and implement support to local forces. This necessity to rethink OMPs is all the more important since certain choices regarding capacity in the current model of the "direct contact" land army[21] seems, at a first look, not very compatible with the requirements of compound combat[22]. The final

21. This new organization, implemented since 2015, aims to adapting itself to changes in the world and in threats. It establishes a new architecture for the army, one that is more flexible and dynamic, organized around thirteen commands.

22. For example, the VBMR Griffon was conceived for high-intensity engagements. It was not designed to be easily transported by air between African countries or to perform somewhat autonomously within a local troop. Similarly, information development and collaborative combat are not priorities in compound warfare.

developments in our paper will therefore try to propose a few paths of reflection that would permit the increase of efficiency in our support of our partners.

Combating a Double Belief

Thinking about the actions of OMPs first requires that we renounce two inhibiting beliefs that are unfortunately, widespread.

First, we must resist the idea that OMPs are "easy, armies have always been putting it into practice". Certainly, the repeated training in shooting and combat given in Africa for decades could be incorporated into OMP actions. Far from being the alpha and the omega of those, they are only the expression of the simplest, least successful among them. In the same way, it's useless to consider OMPs only through the lens of culture. A troop, in order to effectively help an allied army, should not content itself with learning expressions of courtesy in the local language. We must repeat: lawsuits brought against OMPs for ineffiency most often come from a confusion about the different kinds of OMPs, which we have just outlined here. The structural OMP allows us to expect structural results, never short-term tactical victories. In this way, creating a support base company and sending it into battle alone, without compounded units, is, in general, synonymous with defeat[23].

23. The Senate report previously cited brandished "the Chad

The second belief is the idea that short-term operational military partnerships (compounded combat) would be the exclusive domain of special forces (SF). If the many qualities possessed by SF predispose it to this kind of action, it's perfectly false to conclude from this that they should monopolize it, for these three main reasons. Firstly, if SF have exclusive rights over the actions of short-term OMPs, we would be depriving ourselves of the mass effect, since the weak numbers of SF do not allow for the bringing on of a significant number of foreign troops. Next, if SF are absorbed by OMP actions, the force deprives itself of other capacities which are out of reach for regular troops. Thirdly, certain kinds of OMPs, notably compound combat, require, above all, the skills of regular fighters. This means that the frameworks of artillery or engineering units will always be conducted more effectively experts in this area, rather than by commando units that have been hastily trained with equipment that they have not mastered.

In short, as the policy document "Future Land Action" reminds us, OMPs "although similar in form [...] do not come under either special or clandestine operations but rather, a fundamental expertise in land forces."

---

example" to demonstrate the positive results of structural and operational cooperation. There's still reason for skepticism since Chad's promising results in northern Nigeria were, above all, due to their culture of war and their unrestrained use of violence.

Thinking of OMPs in a System: Food for Thought

OMPs should be the study of increased study, at all levels, lest they be thought of the "side-kick" to real operations.

Firstly, on the strategic level. We have attempted to demonstrate in our chapter on armed mediation that strategically, there's a difference between helping a partner win by supporting them and waging war and winning it in their place. In the first case, the intervention can be synonymous with rebalancing the local political landscape if it is properly thought about. In the second, it seems more like a massive political earthquake, leaving more questions than answers. It is therefore urgent to think about the political and strategic role of the OMP, as a first area of study.

After having conceptualized the strategic role of an OMP, it's essential to think about how they're implemented so that the units leading them have a clear understanding of what they're doing. The "OMP ideology" will therefore have to, before anything else, establish a conceptual frame. To do this, there are many big questions that must be approached.

Reflection on Structure

The first question is that of structure. A unit that is engaged in combat does it always by structuring, or organizing, its different units in a specific way. Let's take an example: if tomorrow, an infantry company and an artillery battery get put on a mission to support G5 units, it's a safe bet that, in the current state of our engagement standards, the organization will be limited to inserting a few connecting elements amongst partner units, and that the combats will take place following two distinct chains of command: a French chain on one side and an African chain on the other. This option has the advantage of remaining relatively easy to lead but the support of African units remains less than optimal. The compounding can be thought about in a much more ambitious way. It means going further into integration and diagnosing the needs of friendly units and injecting, in the hearts of their units, a few key capacities: without radically changing the natures of the units themselves, these new capacities would allow them to get the upper hand over the enemy. It means, for example, detaching an anti-tank piece in order to destroy a pick-up truck 2000 meters away, inserting mortar in another place to destroy a checkpoint 4000 meters away, inserting an advance air controller to strike a column that is exfiltrating itself... In the absence of real reflection about the way to intertwine regular fighters in partner units, compounding will always be greeted with skepticism. We will first cite the problems of interoperability in order to explain that this kind of combat is unrealistic. We will also underline certain dangers, our partners not always having mastered at their weapons. Certain people will even say that fighters in regular armies are not autonomous enough! The experience of the colonial wars, the OMLT[24] or the French gunners and sappers in the Levant, today, allows us to prove the contrary. Naturally, compounding is often blamed for the risks that it compels inserted units to take. This risk is real but it is also qualified with other benefits: an inserted presence is not on the front lines and therefore, enjoys the protection of a first layer of local troops, in case of ambush or IEDs[25]. Experience also shows that mastery of the field and understanding of local actors are the best guarantees against unforeseen attacks and other nasty surprises. In short, if compounded combat represents, without hesitation, an organizational challenge for regular units, it is nonetheless not out of reach. Important work in ideology must be done. What is the level of "scale"[26] of a regular unit? How do we define the "unsinkable"[27] unit in compounded warfare? What command architecture should we choose? How do we think about the compounding of a combat unit (a joint tactical sub-grouping) within the volume of one or two partner regiments? How do we think about the support of a compounded unit?

24. OMLT: Operational Mentoring and Liaison Team - In Afghanistan, this meant building units with half-a-dozen people each which were integrated into the battalions of the national Afghan army to improve their operational level.

25. Improvised Explosive Device

26. Scale: a problem faced by French units inserted within foreign troops: what is the minimum size that these small detachments can have? We also sometimes refer to "unsinkable pawns".

27. In military language, an unsinkable element is a unit whose volume and means are enough to be able to face a threat with no risk of being submerged.

This reflection also encourages us to think about the rise in power of designated units. A kinematic type should be imagined. The French experience with OMLTs in Afghanistan has allowed for the extracting of three big phases for partnership missions: an auditing phase during which an experienced detachment assesses the need for a partner, the deployment of a first attachment to evaluate the situation, then the reactive adaptation[28] of the following detachments to always stick to the changing needs of the partner. This kinematic type, which has been satisfactory, would merit consolidation so that engagement in a partnership would be more comprehensible to soldiers who often have the impression of improvising when accompanying a partner.

Aspects Regarding Capacities

To support such units, we must think about capacity. Regular units, in our model of the current army, are immense breeding grounds for equipment, be in the means of aggression, at short or long distances, or the means of seeing or acquiring. As such, the main aspects of key abilities to support a partner already exist. Certain deficiencies remain however, notably in the area

28. This reactive adaptation is obtained in different ways: operational emergency purchases, reports of experiences in short loops, the training of "future" mentors by "former" mentors, the setting up of operational assistance detachments, etc.

of satellite transmissions[29] and in all likelihood in the area of mobility[30]. But beyond these shortcomings in capacity, regular units would need, to partner together effectively, a certain amount of minor equipment, which taken individually, would be too tiny to be taken into account in military planning law, which tends to favor more substantial programs. It would make sense, just like in the SCORPION program, to think of the capacity needs of OMPs as a whole, so that the sum of "minor equipments" can build up a whole that is coherent in terms of programming and financing.

Still in the area of capacity, a light "deregulation" would be equally necessary to adapt itself to the nature of the partner. In fact, if tomorrow, a French unit is partnered with an African unit, which didn't have enough weapons or fuel, not only would their presence be inefficient, but these deficiencies would also represent a threat to the safety of our soldiers[31]. Relying on the supply chain of the partner wouldn't make much sense since the supply chains of our partners are still more damaged than their combat units. It would be necessary for the partnered units to have a certain financial

29. Americans have purchased transmissions from Thalès for their future OMP units.

30. A small, multipurpose, armored vehicle would be a lot more useful than armored medians.

31. Three hundred armed soldiers, even if their shooting is not very precise, can be effective as protection.

autonomy[32] in order to contribute to the purchasing of fuel or small mechanical parts. They would also need to be ready to supply a part of the weapons which the partner would need in order to carry out its missions, if only for the protection of inserted units[33]. The question of a certain deregulation also poses itself in the area of helping foreign units. For a western unit partnered with a foreign army, the objective is not only to bring a few key abilities but also to make the partner's units effective. If the bringing of key abilities does not present too many issues, the optimization of what the partner brings is today left to the judgment of the inserted soldiers. In accordance with their experiences, certain will manage to adjust to the partner armies. Certain artillerymen in Afghanistan have even managed to render artillery guns more effective by learning, in situ, how to use artillery guns that they'd never used before. To allow all engaged soldiers to acquire the necessary experience to optimize their use of their partners' weapons, two actions are possible. The first would consist of buying the most common light weapons in commercially available off-the-shelf packages in order to build a pool of them in

32. The ability to locally purchase fuel, to emergency purchase local food, to settle different daily eventualities that, without money, quickly become major obstacles

33. The transfer of ammunition is strictly dictated by international law; in any case, this does not mean fitting out large battalions but contributing locally to the protection of our troops.

teaching centers[34] and training camps[35]. A second could be to approach our partners in Eastern Europe to be able to organize, in their training camps, sessions where our specialists could familiarize themselves with the equipment of the former Warsaw Pact. These innovative partnerships would be a useful way to involve certain of our European neighbors, who would in all likelihood be welcomed by small countries looking to tighten the bonds with Western Europe; this is especially true in the specific context of Russian interference in the Balkans.

Partnering and International Coalitions

What would be the place of our allies in such interventions? At a time when we are trying more than ever to work in coalitions, as much for reasons of legitimacy and capacity as for those of cost, our thoughts might seem out of step. As it were, the principle of armed mediation presupposes a French decision-making autonomy that is inconceivable within the framework of a classic coalition. In the same way, the driving of a compound war is possible with certain countries like the United States in the Levant; it remains impossible with others like Germany. For these reasons, the principles of ad

34. This especially refers to the Detachment for Operational Support in Canjuers, which specializes in training units before they are sent off.

35. Incidentally, these weapons would justify the purchasing of ammunition.

hoc coalitions should continue to be prioritized in our zone of influence. In addition to the support of traditional partners, more innovative collaborations could be looked for. We have already brought up this idea in the framework of familiarizing our soldiers with the use of foreign weapons, especially those from the former Soviet Union. Another project might be initiated with the United Arab Emirates (UAE), Brazil or South Africa in relation to the issue of African air force. Despite all the willingness in the world, it remains difficult to create the essential air tools that would allow African countries to exercise their sovereignty on their own territory. The few aircraft concessions (a few Gazelle helicopters in Niger, for example) often take on the appearance of poisoned presents[36], since the issues surrounding their support are complex. Additionally, the French defense industrial and technological base (DIB)[37] has no expertise in the low cost small fighter planes dedicated to counterterrorism; French manufacturers have not chosen to invest in this area. Conversely, three of the aforementioned countries are currently developing a real expertise in this area. If we take the example of the UAE, after having purchased low cost American fighter planes off-the-shelf and seen their operational added value, today they are throwing themselves into

36. The devices that we pass on are antiquated, with spare pieces missing. As such, we are contributing to the creation of a series of micro-parks, filled with perfectly inefficient machinery.
37. This refers to the industrial and technological base for defense.

the production of aircraft that seem paradoxical when you look at the usual criteria for a fighter plane but which are perfectly adapted to compound warfare: at the cutting edge of technology concerning weaponry and optronics, they are built around a frame resembling those found on small planes meant for tourism. As a result, they are immensely less expensive than traditional fighter planes, the rustic character of the basic cell and the thrust being deliberately preserved[38]. In the theaters of engagement where the enemy has neither fighter planes nor anti-aircraft defense, this equipment would be perfectly adapted and our partners could seize them immediately, as much in the technical field as in the operational field.

What could our desired partnership look like? France could supply aeronautic specialists who would take created units and train them and accompany them on operations; the UAE and other financial powers[39] could finance the bulk of the project, finding in this way an opportunity to export their industrial flagships, today eclipsed by American competition. This example of fighter planes at low prices in which certain countries invest might seem anecdotal, however it allows us to underline two things: first of all, it's the complementarity of capacities that should outweigh the show logic in the choices of our partners; second of all, there is frequently more to expect from "small countries", who

38. Jennifer Dybman, *op. cit.*
39. Provided that religious compensations are not requested

are often more imaginative and pragmatic, than our big allies, who are generally speaking, less adaptable.

Partnering and Ethics

Finally, the ethical framework of our partners deserves particular development. Inserted among the ranks of a foreign army, western soldiers find themselves with fighters who do not have the same war traditions, nor the same relationship to violence. This is a delicate situation. If it is pointless to want to impose western standards of using force, it is no more acceptable to become complicit in abuses, under the pretext of efficiency. Although no miracle solution can, in all likelihood, be found for this ancient question[40], thinking about it is necessary so that our willingness to limit useless acts of violence is expressed in a rational way[41], without waving about moral arguments, which, at the heart of the free-for-all, would not be very persuasive. In any case, a principle of lines not to be crossed, wisely chosen, should prevail.

40. Clausewitz wrote: "[...] it's useless, absurd even, to rule out the nature of the brutal element because of the repugnance it inspires. If the wars of cultivated peoples are less cruel and destructive than those of uncultivated peoples, this holds with the social situation of the states, as much amongst themselves as with each and every one of them." – from Carl von Clausewitz, *De la guerre, op. cit.*

41. The necessity of not executing prisoners is more easily explained by arguing for the need to demonstrate strength rather than by waving around international conventions.

At the end of this long digression on the actions of partnerships, the courageous readers who will have followed this reasoning might legitimately wonder if this interest in partners and the contemporary range of the indirect approach, does not speak more to military mythology rather than military efficiency. Three observations will, nevertheless, explain our insistence. First of all, today, certain peoples support less and less interventions from foreign powers, whether or not they have UN mandates. The idea of "coming to someone's aid", rather than "imposing" therefore has a future to the extent that it allows people to better accept interventions. Next, at a time when the entire infantry could be united in France's largest stadium, the question of partnerships is essential. Even in high-intensity engagement with a balanced enemy, our armies are far too small to be able to count solely on an autonomous engagement with their heavy means. A certain kind of hybridization of our armies will be necessary, as Christophe Niquille highlights in his excellent book, Pour une hybridation des armées[42]. The OMPs have, in this respect, a great deal of relevance at a time when French families are less and less ready to see their children die for far-off causes.

42. In his work, Christophe Niquille cites an essay by Guy Brossollet, entitled *Essai sur la non-bataille* (Belin, 1975), where, in the heart of the Cold War, he was already proposing this kind of hybridization in order to better absorb the shock of a possible Russian invasion.

Conclusion

What is easy is false, what is complicate is unusable.
Paul VALÉRY

How can we evaluate and improve the efficiency of interventions? The first obstacle that arises is that of the legitimacy of even asking it. An officer could pass judgment on the productivity of an operation without appearing to lack loyalty or perspective, without confusing his emotions with state policy. The question is even more complicated because, of course, there are no objective criteria. Success on the ground might paradoxically lead to strategic failure or might have disastrous political consequences. Additionally, the notion of success can be evaluated differently depending on the time period, which makes this exercise still more difficult. Finally, as political objectives are not always circulated, it might seem presumptuous to judge the efficiency of an operation without knowing those objectives. All of these obstacles could lead to a kind of fatalism; a feeling of abandonment that would limit the military in its carrying out of "skill development", without really understanding the remote objectives, while waiting for a political "reframing" if necessary. This vision might be valid if only minor issues were at play, if operations did not ultimately enter into the future of nations. Engagements in the last decades, which have been on a relatively smaller scale, could let one believe that this was the case. The frequency with which engagements succeed each other, notably in Africa, sometimes gives the impression that interventions fall into a kind of routine; no matter the results of the operations, the intervening countries would not suffer their consequences in terms of domestic policy and the countries that were objects of the intervention would in the end bear no grudges. This thought calls to mind multiple observations. First of all, the use of force is never trivial and, without falling into pointless moral musings, caution should remain the rule when it implicates human lives; the result is that interventions must aim for greater efficiency in order to attain objectives more quickly. Next, the use of force remains an effective means for giving advance warning about and settling conflicts; it would be naïve to imagine that diplomacy is enough and that we can squander the use of armies. In the end, a geopolitical assessment tends to show that France has a huge strategic interest in the success of its operations: it needs to have stable allies, benefit from safe commercial outlets and secured access to the resources that it needs and to control the migration flow. For these reasons, it seems legitimate and pressing to continue to take an interest in the question of the efficiency of interventions.

We began this reflection because, as practitioners of external operations, we wanted to explore the efficiency of the operations in which we had participated. We are aware that at first glance, our status in the military does not seem to predispose us to be the most objective judges, given our training to consider efficiency under the specific angle of the legitimate use of weapons. Nonetheless, military contribution to this reflection seems to us crucial; their restriction to the role of "military tool" would be counterproductive. Over the course of writing this essay, it has been surprising to notice that this subject of military efficiency was not very developed in the military community, while it the object of many books in other circles. Firstly in the political world, which finds the political advantage in interventions too weak and which feels regularly robbed of its rights in this area. Next, the think tanks which regularly approach this subject; the recent engagements in Afghanistan, Irak, the Sahel or Libya being inexhaustible sources for thinking about the efficiency of western armies in today's engagements. Finally, our allies, notably the Americans and the British, who approach this subject with a lot of pragmatism and question themselves on this subject.

To try to approach our contribution to this reflection, we started with details of the situations frequently encountered, in trying to vary the perspectives brought to them: political, military and local perceptions. The following step consisted in demonstrating that the structural and ideological bases that underpin these operations were not necessarily adapted to the realities of the operational contexts that we encountered: the comprehensive approach, such as it is implemented, paradoxically does not ensure the efficiency of interventions. As Émile Simpson underlines, "the comprehensive approach has not risen to the rank of strategy but to wrapping, without true consistency: rather, actions more or less linked between them, a stack of metrics."[1] In the face of this remark, which is widely shared, we wanted to show that other tendencies, which often seem fashionable are not themselves exempt from ideology and potential risks. We have then attempted to develop the foundation for what could be a new approach to interventions. Finally, in order to not limit ourselves to the comfortable role of educated commentator, we took a chance on a few propositions that we thought likely to improve the efficiency of interventions. These reflections, which are general, are despite everything, rooted in the reality of current interventions and relied on the example of Operation Barkhane, the principle French operation of the last five years.

At the end of our analysis, what conclusions, regarding the efficiency of external interventions, can we draw? The efficiency of external interventions is an eminently relative element that, in and of itself, can

1. Émile Simpson, War from the Ground Up: 21st Century Combat as Politics (Oxford University Press, 2012)

only be judged in light of the political intentions that underpin it. Because these intentions are never fully revealed and because they change in relation to the hazards of politics, no assessment would truly be capable of solving the debate, except in some extreme cases where defeat and success are evident. These cases are increasingly rare in current interventions, which develop in "grey areas" or become tangled up in religious motives, tribal issues, enemies who are difficult to identify and populations with no internal cohesion. However, the complexity of these situations does not disqualify the use of armed force: very much to the contrary. This last remains one of the most effective ways to exert pressure, express political determination and inspire respect.

Political ambition is the main prerequisite for efficiency in interventions. To this end, the place of politics, its implication in strategy and the leading of interventions must be questioned. For all that, the political implication is not enough to guarantee the efficiency or success of an intervention. Other aspects, particularly of a structural nature, are necessary so that military operations can attain their wished-for objectives. In this framework, armies can equally contribute to improve the efficiency of operations by adapting their strategy so that they adhere to political will. The general blueprint which serves as the framework for interventions, the manner in which processes of reflection and understanding of real life work, as well as the manner in which these reflections are translated into action, all merit review. The frames of reference that are the comprehensive approach and effects-based strategy are too marked by the context of 1990s to remain operational.

This essay ends with a few propositions. The vision of interventions as armed mediation, the embodiment of political power on the ground and the orientation of partnerships with local forces towards compounded warfare could permit, in our eyes, an improved efficiency in interventions.

Is this age ready for reforms?

No, in the sense that the best engine for reforms is the will to pick oneself up after a failure or the feeling of imminent danger; however, today, interventions are globally satisfactory and France can take pride in itself for a reactive and experienced army. In addition, our institutions work and the French are attached to them.

Yes, in the sense that western armies are today questioning themselves about conflict and remain aware that the relative comfort which has prevailed for a few decades could be followed by harder engagements. The ideological works, strategic reflection and renewed interest of our politicians and the population could push us to a taboo-less thinking on this key subject.

Our only ambition for this essay is that it will contribute to this movement.

Bibliography

WORKS

ARON (Raymond), Le spectateur engagé, Julliard, 1981

ARON (Raymond), Mémoires, Robert Laffont, 2010

BEAUFRE (André général), Introduction à la stratégie, coll. « Pluriel » ["Plural"], Hachette, 1998 [re-ed.]

BEAUFRE (André général), Bâtir l'avenir , coll. « Questions d'actualité », Calmann Lévy, 1967

CHURCHILL (Winston), Mémoires de guerre, coll. « Texto », Tallandier, 2013, Volume 2

CLAUSEWITZ (Carl von), De la guerre, éditions de Minuit, 1955

FUKUYAMA (Francis), La fin de l'histoire et le dernier homme, coll. « Champs essais », Flammarion, 2018

GALULA (David lieutenant-colonel), Contre-insurrection : théorie et pratique, coll. « Stratégies & Doctrines », Economica, 2008

GIRARD (René), Achever Clausewitz , coll. « Champs essais », Flammarion, 2011

HUBER (Thomas M.), Compound Warfare, That Fatal Knot, General Editor, 27 juillet 2004.

JULLIEN(François), Traité de l'efficacité, Grasset, 1997

KANTOROWICZ(Ernst), Les deux corps du roi, coll. « Bibliothèque des Histoires » [« Library of Stories »], Gallimard, 1989
LIDDELL HART (Basil), Stratégie, coll. « Tempus », Perrin, 2015
MORIN (Edgar), Introduction à la pensée complexe, Le Seuil, 2005
NIQUILLE (Christophe), Pour une hybridation des Armées, coll. « La Pensée stratégique », Nuvis, 2016
SIMPSON (Émile), War from the Ground Up: 21st Century Combat as Politics, Presses universitaires d'Oxford, 2012
TOCQUEVILLE (Alexis de), De la démocratie en Amérique, Gallimard, 1850
TODOROV (Tzetan), Le nouveau désordre mondial : réflexions d'un Européen, Robert Laffont, 2003
TRINQUIER (Roger colonel), La guerre moderne, Economica, 2008
VALÉRY (Paul), Regards sur le monde actuel, Gallimard, 1961 [rééd.]
CREVELD (Martin van), La transformation de la guerre, coll. « L'Art de la guerre », éditions du Rocher, 2011
VILLEPIN (Dominique de), Mémoire de paix pour temps de guerre, Grasset, 2016

COLLECTED WORKS

ALLISON (Graham) and ZELIKOW (Philip), The Essence of Decision: Explaining the Cuban Missile Crisis, Pearson, 1999 [second edition]

BADIE (Bertrand) and VIDAL (Dominique), Nouvelles guerres : comprendre les conflits du XXIe siècle, La Découverte, 2016

DURIEU (Benoît général), Dictionnaire de la guerre et de la paix, PUF, 2017

QIAO LIANG and WANG XIANGSUI, *La guerre hors limites*, Payot et Rivages, 2003

REPORTS

Senate report no. 794; July 2016. Information report completed in the name of the Committee on Foreign Affairs, the Defense Committee and the Armed Services Committee, to assess external operations. Authors: Messrs. Jacques Gautier, Daniel Reiner, Jean-Marie-Bockel, Jeanny Lorgeoux, Cédric Perrin and Gilbert Roger

Parliamentary report no. 2777 of the National Assembly, May 2016

« Livre blanc sur la défense et la sécurité nationale » [Official Report on Defense and National Security], 2013

« Action terrestre future » [Future Land Action], Armée de terre [Infantry]

ARTICLES

GROS (Philippe), « Volet militaire de la guerre contre l'EI : quelle cohérence stratégique ? », Parolesdactu.canalblog.com

POIRIER (Lucien général), « Stratégie intégrale et guerre limitée », Stratégique, no, 54, February, 1992

DYBMAN (Jennifer), « Les opérations d'influence britanniques de l'empire à l'Afghanistan », Intelligence on line, n° 714 and 798; DSI, n° 134, March-April 2018

Table of contents

From the same publisher

Collection « Champs de bataille »

Joly de Maïzeroy – Alexandre David

Survivre, c'est vaincre – Cédric de Penfentenyo

Collection « Ligne de front »

La réforme ou l'insignifiance – Bruno Alomar

Un sentiment d'inachevé – Jean-Gaël Le Flem, Bertrand Oliva

La place des armes – Maxime Calvet, Damien Appriou, Jérôme Cheyppe

Collection « Feux croisés »

La fleur au fusil – La croisée des mondes 2017

L'héroïsme – La croisée des mondes 2018

Collection « Honni soit qui mal y pense »

Going Beyond Information

ACHEVÉ D'IMPRIMER

Ce livre a été achevé d'imprimer pour le compte
des Éditions de l'École de Guerre
par Lightning Source France,
1 avenue Gutenberg 78310 Maurepas.

Composition et mise en page :
Bärbel Müllbacher.

Typographies :
à l'intérieur, Coline Première et *Cursive*, © Émilie Rigaud ;
en couverture, American Typewriter, Archer, Bell et Futura.

ISBN : 978-2-35673-037-4

Éditions de l'École de Guerre
www.ecoledeguerre.paris

Imprimé en France
FROC030257221019
22479FR00006B/16/P